MW00332956

Masturbation, Autism and Learning Disabilities

LIBRARY OF
CONGRESS
SURPLUS
DUPLICATE

of related interest

Autism Spectrum, Sexuality and the Law
What Every Parent and Professional Needs to Know
Tony Attwood, Isabelle Hénault and Nick Dubin
ISBN 978 1 84905 919 0
eISBN 978 0 85700 679 0

Sexuality and Relationship Education for Children and
Adolescents with Autism Spectrum Disorders
A Professional's Guide to Understanding, Preventing Issues,
Supporting Sexuality and Responding to Inappropriate Behaviours
Davida Hartman
Illustrated by Kate Bragnan
ISBN 978 1 84905 385 3
eISBN 978 0 85700 755 1

When Young People With Intellectual
Disabilities and Autism Hit Puberty
A Parents' Q&A Guide to Health, Sexuality and Relationships
Freddy Jackson Brown and Sarah Brown
Foreword by Professor Richard Hastings
ISBN 978 1 84905 648 9
eISBN 978 1 78450 216 4

Things Tom Likes
A Book About Sexuality and Masturbation for Boys and
Young Men with Autism and Related Conditions
Kate E. Reynolds
Illustrated by Jonathon Powell
ISBN 978 1 84905 522 2
eISBN 978 0 85700 933 3

Things Ellie Likes
A Book About Sexuality and Masturbation for Girls and
Young Women with Autism and Related Conditions
Kate E. Reynolds
Illustrated by Jonathon Powell
ISBN 978 1 84905 525 3
eISBN 978 0 85700 936 4

Masturbation, Autism and Learning Disabilities

A Guide for Parents and Professionals

Mel Gadd

Jessica Kingsley Publishers
London and Philadelphia

First published in Great Britain in 2021 by Jessica Kingsley Publishers
An Hachette Company
1

Copyright © Mel Gadd 2021

All rights reserved. No part of this publication may be reproduced, stored in
a retrieval system, or transmitted, in any form or by any means without the
prior written permission of the publisher, nor be otherwise circulated in any
form of binding or cover other than that in which it is published and without
a similar condition being imposed on the subsequent purchaser.

A CIP catalogue record for this title is available from the
British Library and the Library of Congress

ISBN 978 1 78775 561 1
eISBN 978 1 78775 562 8

Printed and bound in Great Britain by CPI Group

Jessica Kingsley Publishers' policy is to use papers that are natural,
renewable and recyclable products and made from wood grown in
sustainable forests. The logging and manufacturing processes are expected
to conform to the environmental regulations of the country of origin.

Jessica Kingsley Publishers
Carmelite House
50 Victoria Embankment
London EC4Y 0DZ

www.jkp.com

Contents

Acknowledgements

Thank you to Jo Hinchliffe, who initially developed some of the good practice responses to inappropriate masturbation, and to Corrina Williams, Claire Lightley, Corrie McLean and Rachel Clarke for their support in developing this book. This is not just my work but the bringing-together of many threads of good practice that exist within the UK. Also thank you to Jez Shea and Mandy Williams Jones, who, along with the Jiwsi Relationships and Sex Education (RSE) Practitioners' Network, helped develop the initial guidance that has grown into this book.

Preface

Many people like to masturbate and people with autism and/or learning disabilities are no different. What is different, however, is that sometimes people with autism and/or learning disabilities don't know how to masturbate or don't understand that there are social and legal rules around sexual behaviour such as masturbation.

This book brings together various strands of current good practice around masturbation and working with people with autism and/or learning disabilities. The aim of this book is to enable parents and professionals to support people with autism and/or learning disabilities to masturbate if they choose to do so.

About me

I am a youth and community worker and a registered public health practitioner. I have been working as a relationships and sex educator for the last 18 years. I previously worked for the national sexual health charity FPA (Family Planning Association) as projects and training manager and now am the manager and director for Cwmni Addysg Rhyw – Sex Education Company, a social enterprise delivering needs-led relationships and sex education projects. I deliver a range of relationships and sex education projects, working with vulnerable people who don't always access the sex education they need from mainstream sources – primarily vulnerable young people and adults with autism and/or learning disabilities. I also deliver a range of RSE training to professionals and parents, including my popular course on Masturbation and Working with People with Learning Disabilities.

Chapter 1

Introduction

Why write a book about masturbation?

Masturbation. It's a word that isn't said out loud very much. It is unspoken. It is taboo. It is too private to talk about.

Despite the wide variety of settings and clients I work with, I repeatedly encounter common themes and issues that practitioners working with people with autism and/or learning disabilities struggle with. In my work as a relationships and sex educator, it is clear that masturbation is a reoccurring theme, and is usually brought to my attention when someone's sexual behaviour is no longer seen as socially acceptable or private and so help is needed.

Concerns about managing inappropriate self-touching and masturbation are really very common, although it can often feel as if you are the only one trying to deal with the issue at the time. After receiving a number of similar requests for advice and support from different settings, I developed a single piece of guidance that brought together in a single place current law, advice, relationships and sex education curriculum, and suggested good practice to support parents and professionals. This guidance then evolved into training courses for professionals and parents and has now developed into this book.

Some people with autism and/or learning disabilities will

not have the opportunity (for many different reasons) or the capacity to enter into a sexual relationship with another person, so masturbation may be their only opportunity to enjoy sexual pleasure if they so choose. Parents and professionals have to balance the right of a person with learning disabilities to be sexual, with the responsibility for their sexual behaviour not to impact on other people in a negative way. Unless masturbation becomes problematic for someone (or those around them) it is often not considered as an issue or planned for, especially as it is a sexual behaviour that will not cause pregnancy or pass on a sexually transmitted infection if practised solo.

Through this book, I will explore this balance of rights and responsibilities and how parents/carers and professionals can support a person with learning disabilities to enjoy their sexual self without it harming themselves or other people around them.

Terminology and glossary

Within our work with people with autism and/or learning disabilities about relationships and sex education, we use a range of different terms depending on where we work, where we live and what we prefer to use. Within this book, I refer to people with autism and/or learning disabilities or impaired intellectual ability as people with learning disabilities and I refer to sex education as relationships and sex education (RSE). There is a glossary at the end of the book for further information.

The language we use to refer to the people with whom we interact and the work we deliver is ever-changing, but we should always strive to use language and terminology that does not reduce or belittle the different people around us and that shows respect for the person behind the term we use. Don't let jargon put you off either; it is the intention, care and respect with which we work that counts, not the correctness of using the most up-to-date language.

What is masturbation?

Masturbation is defined as the touching and stimulation of your own genitals for sexual arousal and pleasure. Masturbating can often, but not always, lead to someone experiencing an orgasm. As well as being able to masturbate yourself at any age if you want to, you can also masturbate other consenting people over the age of 16 years old who have the capacity to consent and with whom it is legal to engage in sexual activity. This is known as mutual masturbation. Masturbation can involve using hands, rubbing against things and using objects or sex toys.

It is normal for young children to touch their own genitals because it feels nice, because they are exploring their body or because they are doing it as self-soothing behaviour. However, masturbatory activity for sexual pleasure commonly increases during puberty when there is a rise in sexual hormones and also normal curiosity about sex and sexual feelings.

Masturbation is a common human behaviour and having a learning disability doesn't switch that behaviour off. There is no minimum (or maximum) legal age at which you can masturbate on your own and in private, as UK sexual offence laws only look at sexual behaviour that involves or affects other people.

Masturbation is a sexual activity with a long and complicated history. In the past, many cultures and religions disapproved of the behaviour and punished people who engaged in it. Although now regarded as normal and healthy sexual behaviour by many people, it has still to shed its associations with being seen as abnormal or dirty and rude. This can often make masturbation a difficult topic to work with and difficult for people to challenge when required.

Attitudes and values around sexual development and behaviour

Masturbation can be a difficult topic to discuss for some people. It is useful for parents and professionals to reflect on some of the societal messages they received about masturbation as they grew up and whether those messages help them view masturbation as a normal sexual behaviour or not. It is important to try to separate personal views from the messages about masturbation that the person with learning disabilities could learn in order to enable them to live a happy and healthy life. On a training course I was delivering recently, we were about an hour into the course when one of the participants said, 'Oh, we're talking about women too? I thought this was a course on masturbation.' This is still a default value about masturbation – that it is only something that boys and men do – and this needs to be challenged.

With practice, delivering work on masturbation does get easier. Usually the discomfort lies wholly with the parent or professional, as people with learning disabilities who haven't learned social rules about masturbation do not know that it is 'meant to be' an embarrassing topic. My experience is that people with learning disabilities, particularly if young, are happy to engage in work on masturbation, especially if they then know how they can achieve pleasure or avoid 'getting into trouble' over the behaviour in the future.

When working with challenging behaviour it is tempting to try to resolve the issue in the short term, reducing the immediate problematic behaviour, principally if you are working with more than one person at a time. However, focusing only on the here and now can postpone a problem for a later date or escalate the problematic behaviour. Thus allowing a young person to masturbate in the school toilets to 'calm them down', or giving an adult with learning disabilities a 'calming' head massage despite them getting sexually aroused, is unacceptable (and potentially illegal) behaviour, and we look further at this in the chapter on law and masturbation.

Sexuality

The term 'sexuality' is often used to define what gender someone finds sexually attractive. However, there is nothing simple about a person's sexuality; it is broadly everything about you that is to do with your sexual self – gender, identity, sexual orientation, and likes and dislikes. Some of our sexuality is fixed from birth and some of it develops as we grow based on how we are brought up, what messages we are given, what culture and society we live in, how our identity is formed and what relationships we have or don't have.

The World Health Organization (2018) defines sexuality as:

A central aspect of being human throughout life [that] encompasses sex, gender identities and roles, sexual orientation, eroticism, pleasure, intimacy and reproduction. Sexuality is experienced and expressed in thoughts, fantasies, desires, beliefs, attitudes, values, behaviours, practices, roles and relationships. While sexuality can include all of these dimensions, not all of them are always experienced or expressed. Sexuality is influenced by the interaction of biological, psychological, social, economic, political, cultural, legal, historical, religious and spiritual factors.

Masturbation and rights

Being able to masturbate, if you wish to do so, is a human rights issue. Our right to be sexual is enshrined within the Human Rights Act (1988):

Article 8 – Right to respect for private and family life

1. Everyone has the right to respect for their private and family life, their home and their correspondence.
2. There shall be no interference by a public authority with the exercise of this right except such as is in accordance with the law and is necessary in a democratic society in the interests of national security, public safety or the economic well-being of the country, for the prevention of disorder or crime, for the protection of health or morals, or for the protection of the rights and freedoms of others.

We all have the right to masturbate in private. Our right to masturbate can only be intervened with if we negatively impact other people. Parents, carers and professionals are often in the delicate situation of trying to work out how to both empower people and also protect them and others. We will explore these issues in a practical way within this book.

The responsible exercise of human rights requires that all persons respect the rights of others. The application of existing human rights to sexuality and sexual health constitute sexual rights. Sexual rights protect all people's rights to fulfil and express their sexuality and enjoy sexual health, with due regard for the rights of others and within a framework of protection against discrimination. (World Health Organization 2018)

Freedom and independence

A poor understanding of and compliance with social and legal rules about public masturbation and inappropriate touch can significantly limit a person's freedom and social interactions.

If you masturbate in public places it is reasonable to conclude that you won't be allowed independent unsupervised access to public places where other people may see you masturbating. Therefore, allowing inappropriate masturbation can seriously curtail a person's freedom and growth towards independence. It can also significantly increase supervisory or care staffing obligations as often someone will need constant supervision to ensure that they are not putting themselves or others at risk of harm.

Behaviours learned or allowed to develop when a person is young can last a lifetime. Many people, including those with learning disabilities, can be highly resistant to change once they grow into adults. Dealing with inappropriate masturbation in a timely manner can mean that a person with learning disabilities can experience sexual pleasure in private, and not put other people in harm's way. They can then experience freedom and social interactions without the burden of being labelled as someone who engages in inappropriate sexual behaviour.

Masturbation, sexual orientation and gender identity

In the UK, we live in a largely heteronormative culture; this means we generally assume that people are heterosexual and cisgender unless we are told otherwise. People with learning disabilities are as likely to be homosexual, bisexual, pansexual, asexual, heterosexual, transgender, cisgender, agender or non-binary as the rest of the population. (There are explanations of all these terms in the glossary.)

However, do not expect a masturbatory preference to reveal someone's sexual orientation or gender identity. People's fantasy lives are unique and varied and people will use a wide range or a narrow selection of mental stimuli as a sexual turn-on, irrespective of their identity or orientation.

I mention this here as when you are supporting people to masturbate you must not assume they will respond to the same sexual norms or turn-ons as you or your colleagues, and if they do have a sexual turn-on that is outside a heteronormative script, it doesn't reveal anything other than what they may like to think about in private.

Usually a person's sexual behaviour is a private thing and a person can reasonably expect to keep their personal preferences and behaviour private unless they want or have to share this information with others. Ask yourself: can I offer this person the same level of privacy and respect for sexual identity and choices as I would want for myself?

SUMMARY

- Masturbation is a normal human activity.
- People with learning disabilities have the right to masturbate.
- A person's right to be sexual should not negatively impact other people.
- Your private sexual behaviour should be treated with care and respect.
- If masturbation is not private it can impact on someone's dignity and independence.

Chapter 2

Language and Masturbation

Most people are not used to talking about sex and relationships generally, let alone communicating about a very personal sexual activity such as masturbation. In the UK, people are usually brought up to view sex as either rude and dirty or salacious and funny, not something to be talked about calmly and logically.

Our past experiences and current feelings around sex and masturbation will impact on our comfort levels when communicating with other people about these challenging topics. Within mainstream culture in the UK, masturbation is rarely spoken about openly, and if it is mentioned, people often prefer to use slang terms and obtuse language, such as:

- Wank
- Wanking
- Tommy tank
- Flicking the bean
- Five-finger shuffle
- Cracking one off
- Tossing-off
- Frapping.

I'm sure you can add other terms you've heard to this list. I invite you to take five minutes to think about and list all the terms you have heard of to describe masturbation and people who masturbate.

What messages about masturbation do you receive from the language used? Are the terms respectful and sympathetic to self-touch or are they mocking or crude? Do they focus on self-pleasure and sexual autonomy or on the physical act and possible frustration around it? Does the language focus on masturbating a penis, and boys or men? What terms are inclusive of vulvas and female masturbation?

When we talk about an activity in a negative way we give strong messages that the activity itself is negative. However, if we talk about an activity in a neutral way then the other people around us have the autonomy to make up their own minds as to whether something is negative or positive for them.

A top tip I share with professionals who want to engage people in education or discussion about sexual activity more openly is to practise explaining sexual activities in a neutral way – clearly using factual and neutral language and without giving it a negative or positive inflection. This enables you to work to remove any negative personal values from the description and be more open to the experiences of the people you are communicating with. It will also reduce the levels of embarrassment for all concerned.

For example:

- *Posh wank* – masturbating the penis while wearing a condom. This may be enjoyable because of the sensation or because it collects the semen inside the condom, or because a person is practising their condom use.
- *Five-finger shuffle* – using fingers to stimulate the genitals for sexual pleasure.

- *Flicking the bean* – using a finger or fingers to stimulate the clitoris for sexual pleasure.

Try to remove gender from the explanation and just describe the body part and the activity factually. This makes terms more inclusive for different genders, gender identities and sexual orientations. Being inclusive can take practice but you will notice the improved depth of connection you get with people who don't regard themselves as straight, cisgender or binary.

Clear language is also good inclusive practice generally when working with people with learning disabilities and/or autism. Many of these people won't have had the access to different terms around sexual activity or may misunderstand the euphemisms that people use when talking about masturbation and sexual activity. Being precise and factual enables us all to understand clearly what is being communicated so that no one is disadvantaged because the language isn't known or the underlying meaning isn't clear. This has the additional benefit of enabling clear reporting if an unwanted or abusive situation has taken place. Using the proper terms for body parts and different sexual activities means that we can talk to people about the bad stuff as well as the good stuff.

SUMMARY

- Use clear language to describe an activity.
- Be inclusive of different genders and sexual identities.
- Seek support from others if you are stuck with how to explain something. Working together can help us all learn easier ways of talking about the tricky stuff.
- Practise your explanations of difficult topics. Develop a personal script that you can use to explain embarrassing or sensitive topics.

Chapter 3

Benefits and Harms of Masturbation

When people are discouraged or prevented from masturbating, the main arguments against it centre around the perceived physical and psychological harms that it supposedly creates. Past myths about masturbation harms include getting hairy palms, going mad or becoming infertile.

Here we will explore some of the benefits and harms from masturbating.

Benefits of masturbation
Pleasure
Masturbation has the main benefit of relieving sexual frustration and enabling someone to experience sexual pleasure. We have all those thousands of pleasurable nerve endings within easy reach of our hands, so we may as well enjoy ourselves.

Delaying sex with other people
If we are feeling an urge to have sex (feeling horny), masturbating can relieve that urge and enable us to make choices that are not driven by sexual desire alone.

In medieval times, masturbation was seen as an effective method of restoring purity to someone's nature as it purged the body of lust and sexual frustration and reset it to normal levels.

Ownership of our own body and keeping healthy

Being responsible for our own physical self, our body, is an important skill to learn as we grow away from being small children where a parent or caregiver would see our body during bath time and other care activities. As teenagers and adults, other people can support us with the care of the publicly viewed parts of our body, such as face and hands, but unless we receive intimate care then no one else will see our private parts, our genitals, unless we have a sexual partner or we visit a nurse or doctor to get those body parts checked. Looking at, touching and becoming familiar with our genitalia allows us to get to know our body and be able to spot any unusual changes or illness earlier (for example, noticing a testicular lump).

Ownership of our own sexual experience

Many sexual activities are often framed as being embarrassing, dirty or funny, and it can be challenging for someone to take an active role in learning about sex and how it relates to them. Young people are usually discouraged from taking an interest in how to value their own sexual bodies and how to enjoy sexual pleasure for its own sake, not just for reproduction. Many people with learning disabilities are taught only that sex is for making babies and not for pleasure and intimacy as well. Masturbation enables people to safely explore their own sexual pleasure and learn what feels good for them. They can enjoy solo sexual pleasure for its own sake and if they then have a sexual partner, either now or in the future, they can share what they have learned and be more likely to have mutually enjoyable sex.

Pain relief

Pleasure itself has an additional useful function for our bodies. Studies suggest that having an orgasm can reduce our experience of pain and can relieve the effects of migraines (Hambach *et al.* 2013) and period pains. Hormones such as serotonin, oxytocin and endorphins that are released during orgasm can increase tolerance for pain.

A sensory experience

As well as the pleasure gained from an orgasm, many people find masturbation an intense sensory experience. Pleasurable physical sensations, sounds and smells may contribute to this experience.

Sleep improvements

Having an orgasm can help with getting to sleep. Oxytocin and endorphins are released on orgasm and contribute to feeling relaxed.

Stress reduction

'Happy hormones', such as oxytocin and endorphins, are released during orgasm and these can help reduce feelings of stress and anxiety.

Prostate health

It is thought that orgasming regularly can reduce the incidence of prostate cancer in males. A 2016 study (Rider *et al.* 2016) found that men who ejaculated 21 times or more a month were up to 26 per cent less likely (depending on their age) to report prostate cancer at follow-up than those ejaculating only four to seven times per month.

It is safe sex

If a person masturbates on their own, there is no risk of pregnancy or sexually transmitted infections. However, if they masturbate with someone else, known as mutual masturbation, then there is a chance of passing on a sexually transmitted infection from their hands or sex toys touching each other's genitals or sexual fluids.

Relief of behavioural problems
A build-up of sexual frustration can add to or trigger behaviour problems in some people. We have worked with many professionals who report that once someone has had the opportunity to masturbate they are calmer and happier. Due to the 'happy hormones' such as oxytocin and endorphins, which can be released during orgasm, masturbation can have a self-soothing function.

Potential harms of masturbation
Masturbating in public places could mean a risk of prosecution
Masturbating is a private activity; masturbating in public where a person can be seen is illegal and they could be at risk of prosecution.

It may upset or offend someone
If a person wants someone to see them masturbate then the other person should be a consenting adult with whom it is legal to have a sexual relationship, otherwise it will cause people upset and distress and the person is likely to get into trouble.

It can cause trauma and infection to genitals or other body parts
Masturbating too roughly or using inappropriate objects could hurt the genitals. If there are cuts or grazes, they could get infected if not kept clean. It is important to be careful with the genitals and to look after them.

It can be unhygienic if basic hygiene routines are not followed

When a person masturbates, they may get body fluids such as vaginal fluid, semen and faeces (poo) on their hands, sex toys, objects or surroundings. It is important that any body fluids are cleaned up afterwards and that hands and sex toys are cleaned properly too.

It can decrease sexual sensitivity or create a sexual response only to a narrow set of sexual stimuli

Masturbating is different from having sex with another person. When someone is masturbating, they don't need to tell themselves what feels nice and what doesn't. When they have sex with another person, it may take longer to have an orgasm or they may not have one at all. They may reach orgasm quicker than they expect because of the additional stimulus of another person. A vagina or anus will not feel the same around a penis as a hand. A partner may not touch someone's clitoris as well as they do at first.

It can interrupt daily life

If the person is at school, college or work, it is not appropriate to interrupt educational or work activities to masturbate. We would not see it as normal behaviour for a person without learning disabilities either. Repeatedly masturbating or taking too long to masturbate when there are other legitimate requirements on someone's time is not considered to be healthy or constructive behaviour.

It can flag someone up as a vulnerable person

If someone has poor understanding of the social rules around masturbation and they masturbate whenever they want, even in public places, then this will flag them up as a vulnerable person with no understanding of or adherence to legal and social rules. They may be targeted for abuse as they will be viewed by a perpetrator as someone who is easy to manipulate or unable to knowingly consent to sexual activity.

SUMMARY

- Masturbation is a normal human behaviour.
- Masturbation can be good for you.
- Masturbation can also have negative consequences depending on the situation.

Chapter 4

What Else Could It Be?

Imagine the scenario: a young person keeps touching and rubbing their genitals under the desk at school and keeps doing it despite being asked to stop and wait until they are in a private place at home. When someone is repeatedly rubbing or touching their genitals, it is very easy to jump to the conclusion that they are sexually stimulating themselves through or under their clothes. But, self-touch can be undertaken for a wide range of reasons that have nothing to do with sexual gratification.

Sometimes physical conditions or sensory needs that are not about sexual arousal can be missed because we assume that the touch is sexual or primarily sexual. However, all of us will touch our bodies throughout the day for many different reasons. I have explored some of the reasons here but it is important to gently check out that someone is well or not touching themselves for other reasons before assuming they are masturbating. Repeated inappropriate self-touch may be an indicator of any of the following things.

Sensory needs

Sensory needs – whether something is too stimulating or not stimulating enough – are common with people with autism and/or learning disabilities. This can impact on their masturbation and sexual behaviour too. Sometimes masturbating can be about fulfilling a sensory need for its own purpose rather than a sexual need. This is normal and shouldn't be discouraged but the same rules about appropriate masturbation, in public and in private, will still apply.

Occasionally, problems relating to sensory needs and masturbation can arise and each situation should be assessed individually. Sometimes, intense sensory feedback is too much for someone to enjoy masturbating as they would wish to; alternatives to direct stimulation, such as rubbing against pillows or using vibrating mats, can then be explored. Putting personal values to one side and coming up with a solution based on need can be easier than at first thought. For example, if someone enjoys the sensory sensation of ejaculatory fluid on their skin, this may lead them to engage in masturbation at inappropriate times such as when in school or out and about. A simple solution could be to try activities that involve making play slime which can give similar sensory feedback to touch when they are in an education setting or out in a public place.

Thrush

Thrush is a yeast infection that can affect anyone and various body parts but is most common in vulvas and vaginas. Thrush is not a sexually transmitted infection (see next page) but as it commonly affects a person's genitals it can sometimes be passed between sexual partners. Common symptoms of thrush are itching, soreness, a rash of the affected area and a white vaginal or penile discharge.

Threadworms

Threadworms, sometimes referred to as pinworms, are a common childhood condition. Although they mostly infect children, adults (especially those around younger children), can easily pick them up too. A common symptom is a very itchy bottom and/or vagina.

Urinary tract infection

Urinary tract infections affect the kidneys, bladder or urethra. Symptoms can include feeling unwell, weeing more than usual, pain when urinating, lower abdominal pain and cloudy or smelly urine. Older people can display signs of severe confusion too. People may hold onto their genitals to prevent themselves from needing to pee because it is painful when they urinate.

Sexually transmitted infection (STI)

Sexually transmitted infections are passed on from sexual contact with another person or shared sex toys. STIs can be viral (e.g. herpes, genital warts, HIV), bacterial (e.g. chlamydia, gonorrhoea, syphilis) or parasitic (e.g. public lice). Common symptoms include itching, sores or rashes, unusual discharge, pain when peeing, and feeling unwell. STIs are sometimes overlooked as it may be assumed that the person with learning disabilities doesn't engage in sex with other people. However, they may have a current or past consensual sexual partner you don't know about or it could be a sign of sexual abuse.* Sexually transmitted infections don't generally clear up by themselves and they need appropriate diagnosis and timely treatment. Most testing is non-invasive and can be done at a sexual health clinic, GP surgery, young people's sexual health service or via postal testing (depending on where you live).

Balanitis

Balanitis is a skin irritation that occurs on the head of the penis. It is much more common if a person has a foreskin, and can be caused by irritations or build-up of smegma under the foreskin. It can make the penis sore and itchy and will sometimes need medical attention to identify what is causing it and what treatment is appropriate. If it is a bacterial infection, it may require antibiotics.

Tight foreskin (phimosis and paraphimosis)

One problem with a tight foreskin (phimosis) is where a foreskin won't retract over the head of the penis because it is too tight. It can then lead to conditions such as balanitis. It can cause pain and irritation of the penis. Another condition (paraphimosis) is where a foreskin won't return back over the head of the penis after it has been retracted. It can cause pain and swelling of the penis, and emergency medical treatment may be needed as it can restrict blood flow to parts of the penis.

Inadequate personal hygiene

Poor personal hygiene can lead to bacterial infections, which can cause conditions such as balanitis. Being hot and sweaty can also cause irritated and itchy skin around the genital area.

Overuse or inappropriate use of hygiene products on genital area

Over-washing and using inappropriate hygiene products on the genitals can cause irritation and itching. If someone over-washes or uses perfumed products on their vulva or inside their vagina, it can lead to conditions such as bacterial vaginosis or thrush. Only the outside of the vulva needs to be washed, as healthy vaginas are self-cleansing.

Pubic hair
Pubic hair growth in itself shouldn't cause discomfort or itching; however, if someone removes their pubic hair by shaving, waxing or other hair-removal methods then the subsequent regrowth may feel itchy and uncomfortable. Many people, including people with learning disabilities, may choose to remove body hair for a wide variety of reasons. As with other choices, we need to support people to exercise their choice with minimal physical harm or discomfort.

Tight underwear and clothing
If someone has had a growth spurt or put on weight recently their underwear and/or clothing may feel too tight and restrictive. A person may feel the need to adjust their underwear regularly in order to feel more comfortable.

Physical trauma
The genital area can get as easily injured as any other part of the body but we may be more reluctant to admit it or ask for help if we have a genital injury. Genitals can be hit by a ball, jumped on by a pet dog, struck in a physical attack or harmed during sexual contact. Physical trauma of the genitals could be a sign of unwanted sexual activity* too.

*If you have any abuse or safeguarding concerns, follow your workplace or local social care team's safeguarding or vulnerable adult/adult in need of care policy. If you are a family member with concerns, you can confidentially contact your local social services or seek advice from the NSPCC on 0808 800 5000 or help@nspcc.org.uk. If you feel the situation is an emergency, contact the police immediately.

SUMMARY

- Whether masturbation is positive or harmful will depend on the person and the context.
- Intimate self-touch doesn't always have a sexual motivation. Always check that there is not another underlying reason for the self-touch.
- Be aware of your own attitudes and assumptions about the self-touch or masturbation before deciding whether something is positive or harmful and if action needs to take place.

Chapter 5

Physical and Emotional Development

As we develop from child into adult the changes we go through, physically, hormonally and emotionally, are called puberty. This typically occurs between the ages of 10 and 16 years old and this is when most people start to engage in masturbation as a sexual behaviour. Sometimes someone's social understanding and level of independence don't correspond with the physical development of their body, and it can be a shock for a young person who has a moderate or severe learning disability to have a growth spurt and seemingly change physically from a child into a young adult in a short space of time. In fact, the body's changes occur gradually and the whole process, whether we can observe it or not, takes a few years. For some children, puberty can begin when they are as young as eight, and if they don't understand what is happening to them it can be quite confusing and frightening, especially when they are starting periods or experiencing unexpected erections or wet dreams.

It is important that all children and young people are prepared for the changes they will go through before they happen. If children understand why and how their body is changing then they will be less frightened and confused by what is happening to them. They will also be better at managing their new sexual feelings and corresponding behaviour. There are many excellent books and resources available to support puberty education, some of which are listed in the Resources section at the end of this book.

Physical development during puberty

- Body shape changes.
- Pubic hair grows around the genitals.
- Other body hair, such as underarm hair, grows.
- We become sweatier and can develop acne.
- We usually become fertile – ovulation and sperm production start.

Emotional development

- We may experience strong emotions and unexplained mood swings.
- Romantic and sexual attraction to others starts to form, but having no sexual attraction to other people is also normal.
- We seek more independence and autonomy in our lives

Additional female body development at puberty

The female body produces the hormones progesterone and oestrogen, mostly in the ovaries, which start the changes of puberty. There are several changes a female's body goes through during puberty:

- Breasts and nipples grow and become more sensitive.
- The vagina begins to discharge a fluid, which changes colour and consistency over the course of a monthly cycle. This is normal and it helps to keep the vagina healthy.
- Ovaries grow and begin a monthly cycle of releasing an egg which, if not fertilized by a male sperm, is broken down and shed with the lining of the womb. This is known as a period or menstruation.

Additional male body development at puberty

The male body produces the hormone testosterone, mostly in the testicles, which starts the changes of puberty. There are several changes a male's body goes through during puberty:

- Testicles and penis grow larger.
- Testicles start to produce sperm and semen, which can be ejaculated.
- Spontaneous erections and wet dreams (nocturnal ejaculation) begin.
- The voice box grows, which can make the larynx look bigger, and the voice often changes and starts to sound deeper.
- Facial hair and other body hair grow.

Starting to masturbate

It is normal for children to touch and explore their genitals from a very young age, and even babies will grasp their own genitals when in the bath or having their nappies changed. However, most people report that they start to masturbate for sexual pleasure when they are going through puberty. In 2009, the National Survey of Sexual Health and Behaviour surveyed 820 adolescents aged 14–17 years in the USA. It was subsequently reported (Robbins 2001) that up to 78 per cent of males and up to 41 per cent of females masturbate and that masturbation is 'an important component of adolescent sexuality rather than an isolated or transient phenomenon'. More recently, a 2019 Tenga Self-Pleasure Report (Tenga 2019) surveyed over 10,000 people in nine countries around the globe, and reported that up to 91 per cent of people in the UK masturbate. It also reported that the average starting age for masturbating is 14 years old. However, it is worth noting that this is a survey undertaken by a sex toy manufacturer, and given that masturbation is a self-reported behaviour, no single survey will be entirely representative.

Sam has started getting erections at home and at school. He doesn't know why he gets them and what to do, and he is alarmed by them. He has started to carry around a soft toy with him and covers his genitals with it when he gets an unwanted erection to 'make it go away'. He becomes distressed when he doesn't have his soft toy with him all the time. His support worker delivers some puberty education to let Sam know that erections are normal and his erection will subside after a short time. Sam is taught other techniques to hide his unwanted erection when he is in public. He stops carrying around his soft toy all the time as he feels he can cope with the erections better and they cause him less anxiety.

SUMMARY

- It is normal for young people to start to masturbate as they go through puberty.

- It is important for children and young people to be aware of the physical and emotional changes that will take place during puberty and know what to expect.
- It is necessary, therefore, that young people are taught and understand the 'rules' around appropriate behaviour before they go through puberty and start to want to masturbate.

Chapter 6

How to Masturbate

Choosing to masturbate and how people masturbate are matters of personal preference and choice. There are resources and websites with masturbation technique tips for further research, some of which are listed in the resources section of this book. However, an internet search will quickly offer you pornography as well as educational resources, so check out any materials first before you send someone off to look up this information for themselves. Pornography can be useful for some people (over 18s only), but it is worth remembering that masturbation pornography is usually created for the visual entertainment of the viewer rather than the physical pleasure of the person masturbating, so it should be viewed with that in mind.

I often meet professionals or parents who are trying to support someone to masturbate who is a different gender to them: 'I don't have a penis, so how can I teach them to masturbate?' Don't get too preoccupied with gender: people with the same set of genitals will choose to masturbate in a variety of different ways, and it is the underlying messages of choice and pleasure that are important. Also, it would be totally inappropriate for a professional to say, 'I masturbate in this way and this works for me' to the person they are working with. We never, ever talk about our own sexual activity and preferences in relationships and sex education (RSE). Always frame examples of masturbation technique in a distanced, third-person way.

If you are delivering masturbation education then here is some information that you can give to a person with learning disabilities.

Before you masturbate

- Be in a private place such as in your bedroom or bathroom where you live.
- Ensure you have sufficient time to masturbate without being interrupted.
- Create the right environment: shut the door, close the curtains, set the lighting how you like it, minimize distractions.
- If you are using materials such as lubricant, pornography (over-18s only) and/or equipment (for example, sex toys) to masturbate with, have what you need to hand before you start.
- Have some tissues or wipes handy to clean up any body fluids or lubricant.
- Wash your hands before you touch your genitals.
- Make sure your door is shut and, if you use a sign for alone time or privacy, check that it is displayed correctly.
- Remove or undo any items of clothing that you want to.

Masturbating if you have a penis and testicles

- Use your hand to hold your penis and move your hand up and down it. Try out different strength grips with your hand.

- Your penis will usually become bigger and harder when you masturbate. This is called an erection and it is normal. If your penis remains soft and its usual size then you may still enjoy pleasurable sensations by touching it.
- If you have a foreskin, you can hold it within your grip and move it gently up and down and over the head of your penis.
- You can move your hand around your penis for different sensations.
- The head (glans) of the penis has the highest concentration of nerve endings so you can focus on touching there. If that sensation is too much then touch near there but not directly on it.
- Some people like to touch, hold or gently pull their testicles while they masturbate.
- Some people like to touch or gently pull their nipples while they masturbate.
- Try masturbating in different body positions: lying on your back, front, side, sitting up, standing up. Experiment with how this can provide different sensations.
- Lubricant can help with increasing pleasurable sensations and with reducing soreness.
- There are sex toys available for masturbating penises (see the chapter on sex toys).

Masturbating if you have a vulva and breasts

- Use your fingers to touch your clitoris and vulva; try out different movements with your hand.
- You can move your hand around your vulva for different sensations.
- Don't put anything sharp or dangerous in your vagina.

- The clitoris has the most nerve endings so you can focus on touching there. If that feeling is too much then touch near there but not directly on it.
- You can put a finger or fingers inside your vagina. Be very gentle when first starting to try this.
- Some people like to touch or hold their breasts and nipples while they masturbate.
- Try masturbating in different body positions: lying on your back, front, side, sitting up, standing up. Experiment with how this can provide different sensations.
- Lubricant can help with increasing pleasurable sensations and with reducing soreness.
- There are sex toys available for masturbating vulvas, vaginas and clitorises (see the section on sex toys).

Masturbating an anus

- An anus has many nerve endings around it and within it. If you are biologically male and have a prostate gland then this sensitive body part can be felt inside your anus.
- Use your fingers to touch the outside of your anus; try out different movements with your hand.
- You can move your hand around your anus for different sensations. If that feeling is too much then touch near the most sensitive bit but not directly on it.
- You can put a finger or two inside your anus. Be very gentle when first starting to try this.
- Lubricant can help with increasing pleasurable sensations and with reducing soreness.
- Don't put anything sharp or dangerous in your anus.
- There are sex toys available for anuses. Only use sex toys that are designed to be inserted into an anus (see section on sex toys)

- You have to be careful when masturbating your anus; objects and sex toys that are not designed for an anus can be hard to get out again and can cause injury inside the rectum (bottom). If something does get stuck in your rectum, it is recommended that you seek medical advice.
- If you do put your fingers or a sex toy in your anus, don't put them/it in your vagina (if you have one) or mouth afterwards as there may be germs on your fingers or the sex toy. Clean your hands or sex toy carefully first.

Afterwards

- Clean up any ejaculate, vaginal or other fluids and lubricant with tissues or wipes, and put them in the bin.
- Wash your hands.
- Do up your clothes, get dressed or put on nightwear.
- If you have used sex toys or other objects or materials, make sure you clean them properly and then store them away safely.
- Open your curtains.
- If you use a sign for alone time or for privacy, remove it from your door.

Unable to orgasm

Many people with learning disabilities, who do not have access to good RSE and educational material about sex and masturbation, may find masturbation difficult. If you don't know how your body works and what to expect when you are feeling sexual, the whole business can feel confusing and sometimes frightening. This can result in emotional and sexual frustration and/or physical soreness or injury.

There are psychological factors that may prevent orgasm:

- Not knowing how to masturbate
- Guilt and shame around masturbation
- Worry about being seen, especially by someone who would disapprove
- Stress/anxiety
- Past or current trauma, e.g. self-injury or abuse
- Religious/cultural beliefs of self and family
- Lack of privacy and time alone
- Lack of physical and sexual stimulus
- Too much physical stimulus.

Physical factors that may impede orgasm:

- Hormonal disorders
- Physical impairment
- Hypersensitivity
- Illness
- Injury
- Effects of medication.

Learning where and how to touch yourself to give yourself sexual pleasure is a process. Learning that masturbation is normal and that you have the right to a private place and time to engage in it can be a start of this process. Having the appropriate sex education about anatomy and function and what to expect will also help.

Many difficulties with reaching orgasm can be solved with simply providing a suitable lubricant. Water-based lubricant can add to the pleasurable sensations of masturbation and decrease discomfort and chafing.

SUMMARY

- Some people with learning disabilities may not know how to masturbate and may require clear information in order to learn how to do it.
- Some people may have difficulty in achieving orgasm for many reasons. Don't assume it is therefore not possible for them. Work with them to see if they can reduce barriers to orgasming if they want to.

Chapter 7

Masturbating If You Are Transgender

People with learning disabilities are as likely to be transgender as the rest of the population so being aware of some of the particular issues facing transgender people is recommended for anyone who works in this field.

Sometimes people who identify as transgender have body incongruence: gender dysphoria caused by the mismatch between biological sexual parts and gender identity, and body dysmorphia caused by constant feelings that some part of their body is perceived to be wrong and needs to be changed. Not all transgender people will have these feelings and it is also possible to have gender dysphoria and not body dysmorphia, and vice versa. Gender dysphoria and body dysmorphia can sometimes make it challenging for someone to masturbate effectively and this can be an issue for cisgender people too. To experience sexual pleasure from a body part requires a certain amount of acceptance around that body part, and if you don't feel that you own, belong with or like your own genitals then that can cause problems.

Whether a person wants to touch their own body or not is a personal choice, and there are some techniques they can use if they want to masturbate but find their body incongruence blocks their enjoyment of masturbation.

Renaming the body parts

A person can take ownership of their body parts by renaming them to suit the body image that they have or want for themselves. Although in relationships and sex education (RSE) I recommend we learn the correct terms for our anatomy, there are no rules against creating our own terms for our own body parts and genitals as well. Many people already have alternative and personal names for their private parts.

Reducing visual barriers

Masturbating while either fully/partially dressed (or while wearing knickers, pants or nightwear), or masturbating over the top of clothes, can reduce dysphoria and be enabling. Masturbating under the bed covers or in a bubble bath are also a suggested option to avoid visual feedback that is discouraging.

Hands-free masturbation

Rubbing the genitals against something such as a pillow can stimulate a person pleasurably without requiring hands-on genital touching which may increase dysphoria or dysmorphia.

Using sex toys

Not directly touching genitals with the hands but with a sex toy may help. There are also specialist sex toys for transgender people, whether they are undertaking transitioning interventions or not.

Masturbation Flowchart

You want to masturbate...

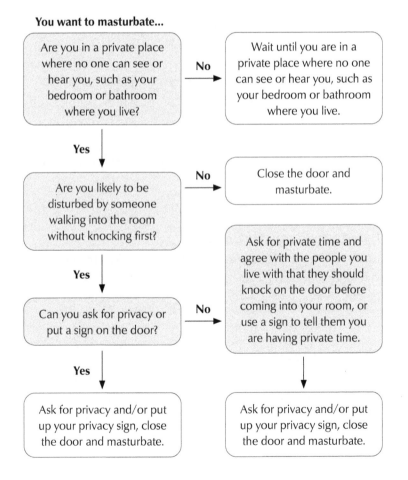

Public and Private

Understanding the concepts of public and private are the bedrock of successful work in this area:

- Public and private parts of the body
- Public and private places/locations.

Private parts of the body

Private body parts are the parts that are normally covered by underwear or a swimsuit. Alternatively, we can define them as being the parts of the body that menstrual blood, vaginal discharge, semen, poo and wee come out of, and also a person's breasts. If a person is receiving personal care, a caregiver will have to touch their private parts, so an explanation of different types of touch will have to be incorporated into any masturbation education.

Just because we have private parts of the body, this does not mean that all the other parts of our body are freely available for others to touch. We can still give and withdraw consent for touch in other areas as we so choose.

Public parts of the body

Public body parts are the parts that are uncovered and which other people can see clearly. In the UK, these body parts commonly (but not always) include faces and hands. Other body parts such as arms and legs may be public depending on personal choice, clothes worn, weather conditions, religious dress and so on. Public parts of the body may be seen by anyone, or a section of people, but still should not be touched by other people without consent.

Public and private places

In teaching about appropriate behaviour, it is important to be clear and consistent about where public and private places are:

Private places: Your bedroom (if you don't share it with anyone else) where you live or are staying; your bathroom at home

Public places: Everywhere else

If a person is living in residential accommodation or staying away from their usual residence then 'your bedroom' will mean the bedroom that they sleep in and don't share with others:

- Private bedroom at home
- Private bedroom at usual accommodation
- Private bedroom in respite care
- Private bedroom in a hotel
- A private bathroom (with a bath or shower) at their accommodation where they can lock the door and spend an accepted amount of alone/private time.

All of the above places must have some agreed rules about entry and privacy. If someone can walk into a bedroom unannounced, whenever they want to, then that bedroom is not a private space. Set mutually agreed boundaries such as placing a sign on the door, having a lockable door, or a rule that people knock on the door before entering.

Signs should avoid saying 'Private'; better they say a mutually agreed phrase such as 'Alone Time' or 'Knock before entry'. This is to avoid confusion with 'Private' offices and 'Private' signs when out and about.

The following are *not* private places:

- *Toilets at school/college/work* – as others can hear or sometimes (as with urinals) see a person using them. Enabling, allowing or turning a 'blind eye' to people masturbating in school/college/work toilets is inappropriate and additionally could be seen as facilitating a sexual offence (see the chapter on law and masturbation).
- *Shared bedrooms* (with siblings and others). People with shared bedrooms should negotiate some sole-use time, using a mutually agreed timetable and sign on the door. Bedrooms shared with sexual partners are considered private places but it may still be necessary to negotiate alone time if the person wishes to masturbate solo without being seen.
- *Rooms labelled 'Private'*, for example someone's private office in a workplace or residential home.
- *Public toilets*. Although the private activities of pooing and weeing can be done in a public toilet, these toilets are not private enough for masturbation or other sexual activities. People may be able to hear or see, even if the person is really careful. It is also illegal to engage in sexual activity in a public toilet (see the chapter on law and masturbation).

- *Family rooms* (other than the bathroom) in a shared home, such as the living room or kitchen. If the person lives on their own or only with their sexual partner they can treat all the rooms as private if no one can see or hear what they do in them.
- *Anywhere someone can been seen or heard* (besides a consenting sexual partner if both are over 16).

It is good practice to build education about public and private into everyday activities to reinforce learning for the whole of life. So when you are in the classroom, out on a trip, on a residential trip or visiting the doctor, ask 'Is this a public place or a private place?' It takes seconds but the benefits can last a lifetime!

Public and private behaviour education

Public and private education activities are an effective way to approach the topic of where to masturbate in private without stigmatizing the person or the behaviour. I never deliver masturbation education without including public and private information and activities as it is essential knowledge. Examples of suitable activities are included in the chapter on masturbation education activities, and additional educational resources are included in the Resources section.

Dan is allowed to masturbate in the disabled toilet in school and a staff member stands outside to make sure no one goes in. Dan recently masturbated in the disabled toilet in the supermarket while his mum was at the till. He didn't lock the door; someone walked in on him and he got very distressed as he has been taught that disabled toilets are private spaces. His mum challenges the school about the incident, and that Dan is allowed to masturbate in school. The school decides to develop a masturbation policy and provides all the staff with training on the issue. Dan is provided with education on public and private places and now knows to masturbate only in private at home.

SUMMARY

- Keep public and private rules simple.
- Public toilets, including school and college toilets, are *not* private in law for masturbation, and it is illegal to masturbate in them.
- Facilitating a person to masturbate in a public toilet or public place is inappropriate and could be considered illegal.
- Masturbating in a private place is a normal part of being human.
- There are good educational resources to help with this issue.

Chapter 10

Law and Masturbation

The Sexual Offences Acts within the UK (Sexual Offences Act 2003 (England & Wales), Sexual Offences (Scotland) Act 2009 and The Sexual Offences (Northern Ireland) Order 2008) set out clear laws around sexual behaviour. These laws are in place to protect people, and behaving within the law is part of our responsibility when we wish to engage in any sexual activity, including masturbation.

This chapter isn't a definitive guide to all laws that relate to masturbation within the UK but rather highlights how someone who is masturbating inappropriately could be criminalized for their behaviour. Much weighs on the interpretation of the law and whether it is in the public interest to prosecute someone, especially someone with learning disabilities. However, as professionals and parents it is part of our role to ensure that vulnerable people within our care don't unwittingly find themselves in a difficult or illegal situation. It is also important that we don't 'bend the rules' because someone has a learning disability. This can significantly impact on their freedoms and rights and also the rights of other people around them.

It can be tempting to get hung up on the interpretation of the law (for example, 'I don't think it is illegal so does that mean I'm allowed to do it?') but use your common sense. Ask yourself if the masturbatory behaviour that you are dealing with would be appropriate if any other member of the population did it. If it isn't acceptable for every other member of the population to do it then the person with learning disabilities shouldn't be enabled to do it either.

Masturbation is not illegal and, unlike other sexual activity, there is no minimum age you have to be to lawfully masturbate. However, engaging in sexual activity, including masturbation, does come with some responsibilities and boundaries.

Some definitions used within the laws around sex

Consent

A person consents if they agree by choice, and have the freedom and capacity to make that choice (Sexual Offences Act 2003).

'Consent' means free agreement (Sexual Offences Act (Scotland) 2009).

What is 'sexual' (Sexual Offences Act 2003)?

Penetration, touching or any other activity is sexual if a reasonable person would consider that:

a. whatever its circumstances or any person's purpose in relation to it, it is because of its nature sexual, or
b. because of its nature it may be sexual and because of its circumstances or the purpose of any person in relation to it (or both), it is sexual.

Capacity to consent

Sexual Offences (Scotland) Act 2009, Section 17

A mentally disordered person is incapable of consenting to conduct where, by reason of mental disorder, the person is unable to do one or more of the following:

a. understand what the conduct is
b. form a decision as to whether to engage in the conduct (or as to whether the conduct should take place)
c. communicate any such decision.

Mental disorder

The Sexual Offences Act 2003 uses the same definition of 'mental disorder' as the Mental Health Act 1983, which has now been amended by the Mental Health Act 2007 S1(1) to include 'any disorder or disability of the mind'.

He/him – they/their

The majority of the legislation within the UK pre-2007 is written with masculine pronouns – he/him. An 1850 Parliament Act (Bailey 2020) said that masculine words in legislation are 'deemed and taken to include females' and that masculine pronouns (he/him) would refer to people whatever their gender. Although recent legislation is being produced in gender-neutral language, the UK Sexual Offences legislation uses masculine pronouns so I have rewritten these as neutral pronouns in order to be more inclusive.

The types of behaviour and the corresponding areas of law that most directly relate to masturbation are explained below.

Masturbating in a public toilet

Masturbating in a public toilet, including a toilet at school or college, is illegal. School and college toilets are legally defined as being public toilets because a section of the public has access to them.

Sexual Offences Act 2003 (England & Wales), Section 71

Sexual Offences (Northern Ireland) Order 2008, Section 75

Sexual activity in a public lavatory
A person commits an offence if:

a. they are in a lavatory to which the public or a section of the public have or are permitted to have access, whether on payment or otherwise
b. they intentionally engage in an activity, and
c. the activity is sexual.

Masturbating in a public place

Masturbating in a public place where the person's genitals and/or their masturbating can reasonably be expected to be seen and therefore cause offence to others is considered illegal. This is equally true if the person has a learning disability or not. If there is no intention to be sexual or to shock or cause offence with the behaviour, or if the exposure of genitals is accidental (for example not doing up trousers after going to the toilet), this will be taken into account as the exposure is not deliberate.

Sexual Offences Act 2003 (England & Wales), Section 66

Sexual Offences (Scotland) Act 2009, Section 8

Sexual Offences (Northern Ireland) Order 2008, Section 70

Exposure
A person commits an offence if:

a. they intentionally expose their genitals, and
b. they intend that someone will see them and be caused alarm or distress.

However, these things have to be present for the situation to be considered illegal:

- Exposing your genitals
- Behaving in a sexual manner
- Behaving without the consent of people around you
- Behaving without the reasonable belief of the consent of those around you
- You are obtaining sexual gratification from the situation and/or humiliating, distressing or alarming another person.

Outraging public decency – Criminal Justice Act 2003

The types of behaviour that may be seen as outraging public decency are wide ranging. These include indecent exposure and masturbating or other sexual activities (real or simulated) in public.

Public places and sexual activity

Sexual activity outdoors is not in itself illegal, which can cause some confusion in understanding the laws around public sexual activity. Basically, if someone can see the person and is likely to be caused distress, embarrassment or harm by witnessing their sexual activity then that activity is illegal. If the person is masturbating (or engaging in other sexual activity) somewhere where they reasonably thought, and can use in their defence that they would not be seen by unconsenting people, then that is not illegal. So, in a nutshell: masturbating in a public place where it is likely the person will be witnessed by others is illegal, for example in an urban park on a Saturday afternoon. Masturbating somewhere where no one will witness the person is not illegal. The legality of this situation and a possible prosecution will depend entirely on whether anyone sees the person and they are offended or distressed, and whether their behaviour is reported to the police.

When working with people with learning disabilities, I recommend that straightforward rules around public and private places are thoroughly understood before going on to explore the nuances of the law.

Allowing or turning a blind eye to someone masturbating in a public place

This could be considered illegal if you are a carer, teacher or other member of staff who facilitates someone to masturbate in an inappropriate place, for example giving permission or sending someone to masturbate in a public place, such as an empty classroom or a public toilet, including a school or college toilet. There has to be a personal sexual gratification element to facilitating someone young or vulnerable to masturbate in order for a prosecution to take place; however, you may be called on to prove that you didn't allow the inappropriate masturbation to take place for your own sexual gratification. Therefore, facilitating illegal or inappropriate masturbation may place you at risk of investigation for a sexual offence.

As well as potentially being illegal, if we allow people to masturbate in a public place when they are under our supervision then they will be more likely to masturbate in public places at other times, as the rules about what they should or should not do are blurred.

There is also the danger that if you do routinely allow this practice within your organization or venue you may create an unsafe environment that puts vulnerable people at increased risk from people who do get sexual gratification from enabling young or vulnerable people to masturbate. This could be illegal too if the person masturbating might be seen and cause offence.

Sexual Offences Act 2003 (England & Wales), Section 17

Sexual Offences (Northern Ireland) Order 2008, Section 24

Abuse of position of trust: causing or inciting a child to engage in sexual activity –
A person aged 18 or over (A) commits an offence if:

a. they intentionally cause or incite another person (B) to engage in an activity
b. the activity is sexual
c. A is in a position of trust in relation to B.

Teaching or helping someone to masturbate in a hands-on way

A carer, teacher or other member of staff facilitating someone who has a learning disability to masturbate by touching their genitals directly or engaging in hand-over-hand genital stimulation, even for educational purposes, is illegal. This should never be done.

Sexual Offences Act 2003 (England & Wales), Section 38

Sexual Offences (Northern Ireland) Order 2008, Section 52

Care workers: sexual activity with a person with a mental disorder –
A person (A) commits an offence if:

    a. they intentionally touch another person (B)
    b. the touching is sexual
    c. B has a mental disorder.

Sexual Offences (Scotland) Act 2009, Section 46

Sexual abuse of trust of a mentally disordered person –
    A person, who is involved in providing care services, intentionally engages in a sexual activity with or directed towards a mentally disordered person.

Sexual Offences (Northern Ireland) Order 2008, Section 44

Causing or inciting a person, with a mental disorder impeding choice, to engage in sexual activity –

A person (A) commits an offence if:

a. they intentionally cause or incite another person (B) to engage in an activity
b. the activity is sexual
c. B is unable to refuse because of or for a reason related to a mental disorder.

Someone masturbating in a public place where other people cannot help but observe

This is illegal (see the public places section previously), but could also apply to school or public toilets where there are other people using the facility, especially children and young people.

Sexual Offences (Scotland) Act 2009, Section 5

Person A coercing Person B into being present during a sexual activity –

- without B's consent or any reasonable belief of B's consent
- engaging in sexual activity
- for the purposes of obtaining sexual gratification or causing humiliation, distress or alarm to B.

Exemptions

There are circumstances that will exempt a person from being prosecuted for a sexual offence. These exemptions cover a professional giving advice or treatment to a child, young person or vulnerable person in order to protect them. This exemption will not cover you if you let your pupil masturbate in the school toilet because it will make their behaviour more manageable during class!

Sexual Offences Act 2003 (England & Wales), Section 73

Sexual Offences (Northern Ireland) Order 2008, Section 77

Exceptions to aiding, abetting and counselling
A person is not guilty of aiding, abetting or counselling the commission against a child of an offence if they act for the purpose of:

a. protecting the child from sexually transmitted infection
b. protecting the physical safety of the child
c. preventing the child from becoming pregnant, or
d. promoting the child's emotional well-being by the giving of advice, and not for the purpose of obtaining sexual gratification or for the purpose of causing or encouraging the activity constituting the offence or the child's participation in it.

Fraser guidelines

The Fraser guidelines (BAILII.org 2020) form a piece of legislation for England, Wales and Northern Ireland that relates to contraception and sexual health advice, treatment and the right to confidentiality for under-16s. If a young person who is under 16 seeks sexual health or contraception advice or treatment it can be given confidentially, without their parents or carers knowing, as long as:

- They have sufficient maturity and intelligence to understand the nature and implications of the proposed treatment.
- They cannot be persuaded to tell their parents or to allow the doctor to tell them.
- They are very likely to begin or continue having sexual intercourse with or without contraceptive treatment.
- Their physical or mental health is likely to suffer unless they receive the advice or treatment.
- The advice or treatment is in the young person's best interests.

In Scotland, the Age of Legal Capacity (Scotland) Act 1991 sets out similar protections:

A person under the age of 16 years shall have legal capacity to consent on their own behalf to any surgical, medical or dental procedure or treatment where, in the opinion of a qualified medical practitioner attending them, they are capable of understanding the nature and possible consequences of the procedure or treatment.

Capacity and sexual behaviour

The Mental Capacity Act 2005 (MCA 2005) is designed to support people who live in England and Wales who do not have the capacity to make some or all of the decisions relating to their lives. Northern Ireland's Mental Capacity Act (Northern Ireland) 2016, the Mental Health (Care and Treatment) (Scotland) Act 2003, and Adults with Incapacity (Scotland) Act 2000 cover common issues.

In order to assess capacity, the Mental Capacity Act 2005 identifies five principles that should apply to all actions and decisions taken under the Act:

1. *Presumption of capacity* – it is assumed that everyone has the capacity to make their own decisions unless it is proved otherwise.
2. *Support to make own decisions* – people must be given support and helped to make their own decisions before anyone else can make decisions for them. This would include delivering relationships and sex education (RSE) within a capacity to have sex assessment.
3. *Ability to make unwise decisions* – people can make unwise decisions or mistakes in their own life if they freely choose to.
4. *Best interests* – when deciding something for someone else then it must be done in their best interest.
5. *Less-restrictive alternative* – when deciding something for someone else then it must be the least-restrictive option in relation to their rights and freedoms.

The Mental Capacity Act 2005 also sets out four functional tests in order to assess whether someone has the capacity to consent to something generally. These are the ability to:

- Understand information relevant to the decision
- Retain it long enough to make a decision
- Evaluate and weigh up the information
- Communicate the decision.

In order to legally be able to consent to sexual activity with other people you have to have the capacity to give informed consent. Not everyone with learning disabilities will need to undergo a capacity assessment as there is presumption of capacity, as set out in the Mental Capacity Act 2005. However, if there is any doubt about capacity or concerns about safeguarding then an assessment on the capacity to give informed consent to have sex will typically include that:

- You understand what the activity you are to engage in is.
- If you engage in heterosexual vaginal penetrative sex there is a risk of pregnancy.
- There is a risk of sexually transmitted infection transmission when engaging in sexual activity with another person.
- You and the other people involved have to consent fully to everything you do and can withdraw consent at any time.

Section 27 of the Mental Capacity Act 2005 makes it clear that no one should make a decision for someone else about what sexual activity they should or should not engage in if they have the capacity to consent. If a person doesn't have the capacity to consent to sexual activity, as proven by a capacity assessment, then decisions made to prevent them engaging in sexual activity will be part of a safeguarding procedure and the avoidance of a potential sexual offence.

In relation to masturbation there is no issue regarding capacity within solo masturbation as there is no sexual contact with other people. Capacity issues could apply here when decisions such as providing sex toys, and providing access to or blocking use of pornography or sex workers, are being undertaken.

SUMMARY

- If you allow or enable a person with learning disabilities to masturbate in a public place or which other members of the public (especially children) have access to, such as a school, college or public toilet, you are potentially enabling or committing a sexual offence and placing the person with learning disabilities and yourself at risk of investigation and prosecution.

- Allowing someone to publicly masturbate or inappropriately touch themselves, regardless of legal issues, reduces a person's dignity, whether they understand this at the time or not.
- A person's desire and impulse to masturbate at the time and place of their choosing does not override other people's rights to go about their daily life without having to witness inappropriate masturbation.

Chapter 11

Faith and Masturbation

As well as the legal rules in our lives about masturbation and other sexual behaviour, we may also choose to follow a range of faith, cultural and social rules guiding us on how we should and should not behave. We may choose to follow different versions of these rules, and each faith and cultural group will have a spectrum of interpretation and adherence to the rules. So an individual faith will commonly have a wide range of responses to masturbation depending on the interpretation and the development of teachings and the perceived impact it has on people.

Each faith group usually has a range of three main approaches to masturbation:

1. It is not permitted under any circumstances.
2. It is permitted if it is the lesser of two evils – for example, it prevents sex before or outside marriage or if you have circumstances in your life that prevent you from getting married to a spouse with whom you can have sex.
3. It is accepted or permitted as normal human behaviour.

Sometimes outdated perceived harms of masturbation are used as evidence that masturbation is bad for you, but these harms have been demonstrated over time to be myths, and there is plenty of good evidence to show that masturbation is normal human behaviour and not physically or emotionally harmful to an individual or to wider society if practised in private. It is reasonable to hold personal beliefs and values about different sexual activities, but if a faith dictates that masturbating is not a permitted activity then inaccurate claims should not be used to support the faith rules.

No demands of faith or culture should harm people, and if you are supporting a person with learning disabilities who wishes to masturbate then it is vital that their overall physical and emotional needs are taken into account. If we believe that masturbation is unacceptable for ourselves then that is our personal choice and interpretation within our faith, but we may find that a different response to masturbation is in the best interest of our child or the person we are working with.

Here is a condensed summary of what some of the main faith groups in the world say about masturbation. Although these are summaries, each faith has a wide range of approaches and responses to masturbation and each person of faith will choose the approach that mirrors best their own internal values and beliefs.

Islam

Although Islamic scripture doesn't specifically mention masturbation (like the Bible), masturbation by your own hand is considered unacceptable behaviour within the Islamic faith. Mutual masturbation within marital sex is considered acceptable. Solo masturbation is sometimes referred to as the 'wedding of the hand'. However, as the age at which people get married is rising throughout the world, and attitudes to sexual behaviour are changing, some Muslims are changing their view on masturbation and identifying it as normal developmental behaviour.

Judaism

The Talmud prohibits male masturbation, for the reason that masturbating to ejaculation 'wastes' male semen. But, there is no official view on female masturbation as there is no semen to ejaculate, and thus waste, when females masturbate. As understanding of normal human behaviour and the realization that masturbation doesn't negatively impact a person's growth, some Jewish groups are becoming more lenient towards masturbation, especially if it helps with exploring sexual pleasure, learning about the body and preventing premarital sex.

Christianity

The Bible (like the Koran) doesn't specifically mention masturbation as a sin, even in the Old Testament Book of Leviticus. However, most branches of the Christian faith teach that masturbation is a sin in response to the story of Onan (see below) or masturbation's associations with lustful and impure thoughts. While some branches of Christianity, such as Catholicism, see masturbation as an absolute sin, some other branches have a more liberal view and see it as the lesser of two evils, for example helping to prevent premarital sex. And some branches of Christianity don't teach that it is a sin at all, for example the Church of England.

Onan

Masturbation is often viewed as a sin by Christian and Jewish faiths because of the Old Testament Bible story of Onan in Genesis 38. Onan's older brother died and God ordered Onan to marry and have children with his brother's widow. If any sons were born from this relationship they would be legally seen as his dead brother's heirs and could claim his brother's share of any family inheritance rather than Onan inheriting it all himself. To prevent the birth of any children, Onan used the 'withdrawal method' (not now recommended as a reliable method of contraception), withdrawing his penis from his new wife's vagina before ejaculating and 'spilling his seed' and impregnating her. This disobedience allegedly angered God, who punished him by killing him. Onan practised withdrawal rather than masturbation but the 'sin' of spilled seed and unproductive sexual acts has become an overarching theme within some religions of only ejaculating semen for the procreation of children. Onanism is sometimes used as another word for masturbation.

Buddhism

Buddhism doesn't give any guidance regarding masturbation for lay people but Buddhist monks and nuns are meant to be strictly celibate and this includes abstaining from masturbating too. Contemporary Buddhism generally sees masturbation as normal human sexual behaviour and as long as it doesn't negatively affect anyone and not become compulsive or be used as a substitute for sexual relationships, it is considered harmless. It is also taught that desire can inhibit personal and spiritual growth so masturbation could contribute to inhibiting this.

Hinduism

Matters relating to sex and sexual behaviour are left to the individual within Hinduism, and there are no teachings relating to masturbation other than that our personal behaviour shouldn't impact negatively on anyone else.

Interpretations within Hinduism range from it being undesirable, as masturbation and associated behaviours (lust, pornography) can inhibit our personal and spiritual growth, through to it being accepted as a normal expression of human sexual behaviour.

Seeking support

As each individual faith will have a range of feelings about and attitudes towards masturbation I recommend seeking support from a range of sources within each faith if an individual, family or professional is struggling with someone's right to masturbate because of their beliefs. In my experience, most faith leaders will place a person's health and well-being above a cultural rule, especially if that person has additional challenges in their life such as a learning disability.

SUMMARY

- Different faiths have a spectrum of attitudes towards masturbation.
- No faith should be detrimental to the rights of vulnerable people.
- Seek information and support from a range of sources within your own faith and culture while developing your own values and ethics about masturbation.

Chapter 12

Relationships and Sex Education Delivered in School

Sex education or sex and relationships education is now known as relationships and sex education (RSE), relationships and sexuality education (also RSE) and relationships, sexual health and parenthood (RSHP) depending on where you live and work.

In the past, RSE typically focused mainly on only stopping the 'bad stuff' that could be a consequence of having sex with a partner or multiple partners, such as unplanned pregnancies or sexually transmitted infections. It was almost exclusively heteronormative (penis-in-vagina sex) and often reinforced outdated values and attitudes towards human sexuality, for example that sex outside a monogamous relationship is riskier sex. Good RSE takes a holistic view of human sexuality and involves learning about the physical, emotional and social aspects of growing up, body awareness, gender and sexual identity, friendships, sexual relationships, reproduction and wider sexual health.

RSE aims to equip children and young people with the information, skills and values they need to have safe, fulfilling and enjoyable relationships and to take responsibility for their own sexual health and well-being. RSE aims to contribute to healthy behaviours, including taking control of reproductive choices, avoiding sexually transmitted infections, understanding and exercising consent, and reducing harmful behaviour such as sexual offences like assault and abuse. Good quality RSE also fulfils children and young people's right to information about their bodies and health.

Recently, there have been exciting developments within RSE delivered at primary and secondary schools in the UK, with RSE becoming recognized as a valuable addition to children and young people's lives and forming a much stronger part of the curriculum. In the UK, education, and therefore RSE, is a devolved area and each country approaches the topic slightly differently. However, in all the countries, the school RSE legislation is inclusive of children and young people with learning disabilities whether they attend mainstream or special/special educational needs/additional learning needs schools.

Northern Ireland – relationships and sexuality education (RSE)

RSE is statutory for primary and secondary schools in Northern Ireland, with guidance given on curriculum content, but schools have the autonomy to design their own RSE programmes. Schools are also required to develop an RSE policy, setting out how they are going to implement RSE for their learners. While there is no statutory parental right to withdraw a child from non-science RSE classes, schools are advised to try to take account of parental wishes.

Scotland – relationships, sexual health and parenthood (RSHP)

In Scotland, RSHP education forms a key part of the Health and Wellbeing section within the Curriculum for Excellence but it is not currently compulsory. However, most schools do deliver RSHP. Parents do not have a statutory right to withdraw their children from non-science RSHP but they can request it, and schools are advised to respect their wishes. The Scottish Government has an RSHP website (www.rshp.scot) full of support ideas and resources, including approaches and resources for pupils with additional support needs (ASN).

Wales – sex and relationships education (SRE) and relationships and sexuality education (RSE)

In Wales, sex and relationships education (SRE) is currently a compulsory part of the basic curriculum for all secondary education pupils, with non-mandatory guidance on curriculum content. Parents currently have the right to withdraw their children from non-science curriculum SRE. Primary schools can deliver SRE but all schools, whether they deliver it or not, have to have an SRE policy which parents are entitled to see.

By September 2022, RSE will be taught across the whole curriculum in all schools, both primary and secondary (but starting in primary initially), and be guided by a statutory code which will set out the themes to be included in the mandatory RSE. Parents will no longer have the right to withdraw their children from RSE lessons.

England – relationships and sex education (RSE)

In 2020, RSE became compulsory for all secondary schools in England, and relationships education (RE) became compulsory for all primary schools, with guidance available for schools to plan their own curriculums. Parents do not have the right to withdraw their children from RE but do have the right to request that their child be withdrawn from non-science curriculum RSE if they wish until the child is three school terms before their 16th birthday. At this point, the young person can request to opt back into RSE without parental consent.

Variation of delivery

Even within the four countries of the UK, there is a lot of variation on how RSE is delivered in both mainstream schools and schools for pupils with additional learning needs. Good RSE should be tailored to the learners' needs so it can be appropriate to their age and developmental ability. Delivering just the basic key stage science or personal, social and health education (PSHE) curriculum can sometimes miss out on essential topics within the RSE range that young people with learning disabilities don't receive or understand without additional support. For example, we often work with children and young people who know all about conception (sperm meeting egg) and reproduction but still don't know what sexual activity or sex actually is, and so don't know how the sperm gets to the egg.

There has generally been a lack of robust education about growing up, puberty and anatomy within the UK. It is common for young people with learning disabilities to not know that boys may get erections, or what wet dreams are. Girls often believe that they pee out of their vaginas and have never heard of a clitoris. A good basic education will help young people understand their bodies and the changes that come with puberty, thus better equipping them to manage and respect their bodies now and in the future. Good RSE can also help protect vulnerable young people from abuse.

A child or young person who knows about their body boundaries, which parts of their body are private, and who is allowed and not allowed to touch them becomes a less vulnerable and compliant target for abuse. And if the worst ever happens, they are much more likely and able to disclose the abuse and get the help they need.

A common issue when delivering RSE to young people with learning disabilities is the focus on the young person's developmental or cognitive ability (sometimes called learning age). I fully agree that RSE should be 'age'-appropriate but it should be physical-developmentally appropriate as well. If a young man has an educational cognitive level similar to a six-year old but he is going through puberty and getting erections then this is a topic that needs to be discussed regardless of whether you would discuss this with other six-year-olds or not.

SUMMARY

- Children and young people with learning disabilities are entitled to good quality and inclusive RSE.
- Parents have the right to access their child's school RSE policy.
- RSE should be tailored to the age and developmental ability of the students.

Chapter 13

Teaching about Masturbation

So it has come to your attention that your child or a person with learning disabilities needs some education or information about masturbation. In this section, we will go through some basic steps that will make this process easier and safer for everyone involved. Masturbation can be a challenging topic to discuss at first. It can be useful for you to reflect on some of the societal messages you received about masturbation as you grew up and whether those messages help you view masturbation as a normal, natural sexual behaviour or not. Try to separate any negative personal views about masturbation from the messages about masturbation that the person with learning disabilities should be given to enable them to live a happy and healthy life.

Many parents and practitioners have concerns about the appropriateness of discussing masturbation with people, especially young people under the age of 16 years old. Are you allowed to deliver work about masturbation? Yes you are, and I encourage you to do so; however, good practice recommends that certain things are in place first.

Is it legal?

Education can be defined as the development of learning, knowledge, skills and understanding, and applying them. It is not only legal to provide timely and appropriate education but it is enshrined within the Human Rights Act 1998, and both the Fraser guidelines and the Sexual Offences Act 2003 make it clear that professionals are allowed to give confidential sexual health education, advice and treatment to young people and vulnerable adults as long as it is in their best interests. 'In their best interests' includes giving advice and education to prevent someone harming themselves or others too. And, of course, there is nothing illegal about parents talking with their children about relationships and sex-related topics.

'Do you masturbate?' – Utilizing distancing techniques when the questions get personal

It is perfectly possible to talk about masturbation without having to talk about whether you yourself masturbate or not. You may get asked if you do masturbate and you can reply with something like, 'That's an interesting question but I'm not here to talk about my private life.' Use distancing techniques to explore masturbation generally. Never share your own experiences as this would be inappropriate. However, you may have to explore your child or client's personal experiences to put the right solutions in place.

Needs assessment

When starting to plan what you need to deliver or what intervention is required, you should initially undertake a needs assessment. This is a vital step. It can be as simple as having a discussion with the person with learning disabilities, or as comprehensive as utilizing questionnaires and consulting with this person and their family, school, college and other staff involved. Your needs assessment will show you what the person with learning disabilities already knows about masturbation and what the gaps in knowledge and understanding are for them. It may even reveal some baseline information that they need assistance with; for example, they do know the rules about masturbation but they don't have a private place to masturbate in or they don't have the confidence to ask for private time. Other barriers to being able to masturbate may be external to them, such as parental views, cultural rules, staff values or sharing a room with a sibling.

Needs assessment methods include:

- Individual or group discussion with or without resources
- Questionnaire – paper or online
- Knowledge or value continuums
- Games or exercises.

Your needs assessment will show you what education and information are needed. It will help you avoid making assumptions based on your own and others' value systems and enable you to tailor the information for the person or the group you are working with.

If you are a professional, you can also take the needs assessment evidence to your manager or team and use it to seek support in designing a bespoke education response for the person or group.

If you are a parent (parents do needs assessments all the time, but they don't usually call it by that formal label), it will help you avoid missing vital information and it will also give you the opportunity to warm up to the subject with your child. 'What do you know about masturbation?' is a great discussion starter!

The setting

Creating a safe space where you can deliver an education session or have a discussion about masturbation is vital. It should be private enough that you can all relax and not worry about being interrupted, but if you have lone-worker boundaries it will need to be near enough to other staff that you can gain assistance if needed. It is impossible to have an educational session about something as sensitive as masturbation if the facilitator or participants are worried about being overheard or interrupted. Put a sign on the door if you need to, pause the session if there is an unexpected interruption, check in with the participants at regular intervals to see how they are feeling, and ask what would make the session more comfortable for them.

Parents talking to their children about masturbation usually find that discussing the topic while doing another task such as travelling in the car, washing up, watching television or being on a walk can help reduce discomfort. Difficult conversations sometimes flow more easily when you are not face to face and feeling cornered. However, this is not a technique that works for everyone so take steps to make time to talk and reduce distractions for that time period.

Some pointers may help:

- Meet in a quiet space away from distractions.
- Make sure other people know not to interrupt you during the session.
- Turn phones to silent and put them away from everyone's line of sight.
- Ensure that you have any resources needed to hand before you start.
- Give a clear framework for what you are doing, for example, 'We are having a chat for half an hour to discuss the topic of masturbation.'

If you are delivering or receiving an education session online it is equally important to create a safe space. Before you start you will need to ensure that you use a digital platform that is secure and safe. You will need everyone involved to be in a space where other people (especially children) cannot overhear them. If someone is supporting the person with learning disabilities to access the online session they will need to be briefed initially as to what to expect so they can support effectively. Using headphones can help keep some of the delivery private, and knowing how to mute audio can block out unwanted noise when you are not talking.

Working agreements

Also known as ground rules and group-work contracts, working agreements are a tried-and-tested group-work technique but can work equally well for one-to-one work too. They are invaluable when you are working with topics that are sensitive and may cause embarrassment and discomfort to either the participant or facilitator or both. Working agreements involve simply setting out some mutually agreed basic boundaries and processes. A good working agreement for masturbation education will include the following aspects:

- *A safe space* – a private space to discuss masturbation where you can't be interrupted or overheard by other people (other staff or family members). Allow enough time for the session, and ensure that the space is comfortable.
- *Respect* – for each other's right to hold different opinions; use respectful language and respect different experiences.
- *Confidentiality* – respecting private information but understanding and implementing safeguarding when needed.

- *Participation* – taking part voluntarily, taking responsibility for your feelings and taking time out if needed.
- *Privacy* – sexual behaviour is private; parents/staff won't talk about their own sexual behaviour.
- *Swearing* – rude/naughty words are allowed during the session in context but must not be used with other people.
- *Touching* – no touching of your own private parts during the session, and no touching other people at any time without their consent.
- *Questions* – questions can be asked, but parents/staff won't answer a question that is too personal/private. The person with learning disabilties doesn't have to answer a question that is too personal/private either.
- *Laughing* – it is okay to laugh and giggle when talking about masturbation. Sexual activity should be fun and talking about it can be funny!

Where to start – parents teaching about masturbation

The good news is that most children and young people tell us that they want to learn about growing up, sex and relationships from their parents and families and those that do are more comfortable in talking about these issues (Sex Education Forum 2011). Parents, carers and other family members are the primary role models for their children. Evidence shows that sex and relationships education is most effective when it is delivered through a partnership between home, school and community.

Starting at a young age

If you ask your toddler not to touch their private parts when you are out in public then you have already started their masturbation education journey. The conscious and unconscious messages that we give children about touching their genitals start from an early age. It is perfectly reasonable to ask your child not to touch their genitals when in public, or in front of the family at dinner, but this can easily be followed up by telling them that they are allowed to do it in their bedroom when they are on their own. It is important to instil a sense of self-ownership over their genitals and for them not to feel shame for looking at and touching their own bodies.

I have worked with many young people who think it is disgusting to look at or touch their own genitals for anything other than washing and going to the toilet. If they feel shame about their own genitals then it will be harder for them to look after themselves properly, to ask for medical help if they need it, to masturbate and experience sexual pleasure on their own, and to experience sexual pleasure with a partner one day. It also can make people more vulnerable to abuse because, if they already associate genitals and touching with shameful feelings, they are vulnerable to keeping negative experiences secret and are less likely to know how to ask for help.

Talking about growing up, relationships, sex and masturbation can become a regular conversation from a young age. Be open to answering questions as they arise; ask them what they already know and what their friends know. Discussing it little and often is the key here – don't turn it into one big talk. Drip feed them with small conversations and regularly repeat the important messages such as public/private, consent and having respect for yourself and others.

Starting when a child is showing signs of puberty

Physical and emotional signs of development during puberty often trigger parents and carers to start discussing growing up, relationships and sexual behaviour. However, just because someone has 'had the talk' doesn't mean that they will have understood it and have covered the topic of masturbation.

It can be easy to leave 'the talk' and the education of our children about relationships and sex until they show signs of going through puberty or being old enough to have the information. But, children go through puberty at different rates, and physical and emotional maturity are not always concurrent. Relationships and sex education, whether at school or at home, works best when it helps prepare children and young people for what is coming ahead, well in advance, so they are not caught out by body changes such as starting periods or having a wet dream, or unexpected feelings and mood swings.

However, even parents of children and young people without learning disabilities don't usually include information about masturbation in their talks with their children, usually assuming that they will pick up on the social clues about this behaviour. Therefore, information about masturbation is often missed out. Think back to when you received relationship and sex education from family and school – did you receive any honest, useful education about masturbation?

By not talking about normal things like growing up, relationships and sex we can unwittingly create a culture of silence in our homes about these topics. If we don't talk about them, children and young people can pick up on the underlying message that they are topics that shouldn't be talked about at home. And if one day they have a question or a problem they want to discuss, where will they go? This can create an unforeseen vulnerability as they may seek out someone else who is willing to talk about sex and this person may not be a safe or appropriate person.

Many parents of teenagers with learning disabilities find themselves in these situations for many different reasons. Usually the main reason is that they are so busy dealing with the day-to-day parenting that looking ahead to puberty and adulthood seems beyond their current resources. It is never too late (or too early) to start talking about growing up, relationships and sex, as we always have something to contribute and learn. In my experience, young people with learning disabilities don't tend to get as embarrassed about the topic as young people without learning disabilities. They will take issues such as masturbation more on face value without the negative value load of the behaviour that young people without learning disabilities have picked up along the way.

Effective conversation starters include:

- Do you know what masturbation is?
- Have you done any lessons about masturbation at school?
- Have any of your friends talked about masturbation? What do they say about it?

Parents of young people with learning disabilities need to be really clear with their teenagers, not making any assumptions about what they know and don't know. I find an enormously wide span of understanding when I deliver educational sessions. Some young people know virtually nothing while others have detailed knowledge that has me searching terms and information after the session to update my practice!

Always try to check in with what your young person knows and doesn't know and work from there. For example, they may be having erections but not know that they are normal, or why they have them.

Starting when your child is an adult

It is never too late to start learning about our bodies, relationships, sex and masturbation. It is common for adults with learning disabilities who have never had sex education at school to know very little about puberty and their own sexual and reproductive functions. My key bit of advice when working with older teenagers and adults is not to make assumptions about what they already know. Again, a needs assessment is vital, and don't be afraid to start at the basics again.

There are some capacity assessments for sexual activity, such as the Sexual Knowledge and Behaviour Assessment Tool from BodySense (see the Resources list), which have checklists for sexual knowledge and understanding. These can be a useful start point with your needs assessment, but these checklists should identify areas for education and learning – not just be a tick-box exercise. I have worked with young adults with learning disabilities who will say, 'Yes, I know what sex is', and then they will say it is 'sleeping together' or 'going to bed with someone', but as they haven't had those terms explained they don't actually know that they are merely euphemisms for sex. They only perceive the literal meaning.

It can feel like a huge responsibility to take someone on their relationships and sex education journey if they have not had any previous education about this subject. However, do remember that relationships and sex education is a process, not an all-or-nothing one-off talk. Give time to the discussion, allow opportunities for them to ask questions, check in on understanding and come back to important points regularly to reinforce understanding. If you treat the topic as normal and approach it with confidence then you will model the approach that a person with learning disabilities can take and the topic will seem natural and easy.

You may not realize it at the time but the most important thing you are teaching is that the person with learning disabilities can talk about this stuff with someone they trust, ask questions and seek help and support if they need it.

Conversation starters for adults:

- Did you have any sex education when you were at school or college? If so, what sort of things have you learned about?
- If not, what do you think you should have learned at school or college?
- Do your friends talk about growing up and body changes? Have they mentioned masturbation?
- Someone mentioned masturbation in that programme we watched last night. Do you know what masturbation is?

Developing a masturbation education programme

An RSE or masturbation education programme will work best when it is developmental and repetitive, giving the participant/s the opportunity to build knowledge and understanding in a logical order and have time to form and ask questions.

A developmental masturbation programme could include:

1. *Introductions*: Getting to know you and why we are here. What do you already know? Forming a working agreement, working towards feeling safe.
2. *Body parts*: Public and private body parts. What are our private body parts? What can they do? How can we look after our private parts? How can we ask for help?
3. *Public and private places*: Which locations are public and which are private?
4. *Public and private behaviours*: Which behaviours can

we undertake in public and which should only be done in private?

5. *Masturbation*: What is masturbation? How do we talk about it? How do you feel about it? How do people masturbate? What do we need to know?

6. *My rights*: What have you the right to do in private? How can we ensure that you can exercise these rights if you choose?

7. *Conclusion*: What have we learned? What else could we learn about in the future? What actions can we all take from this point onwards? Who can help?

As you can see from this example programme, I don't suggest you jump into exploring the issue of masturbation straightaway. It is placed within a logical sequence in the programme, and information on body parts and public and private places is explored first. This provides the context for the learners so that the information on masturbation is delivered at the right point. This is just a suggested sequence, and a needs-led programme will always have the most impact as it will be meeting your learners' unique needs.

A team approach versus lone wolf

Whether you are a professional or a parent, when you are delivering RSE and masturbation education the support of a wider team is invaluable. It is the nature of the topic that interesting and challenging new situations constantly arise, and it is healthy to seek support and guidance from others. Having supportive people with whom you can share concerns or stress can be helpful on a day-to-day basis, and if you are a professional you can access support via supervision sessions at work or practice support networks such as the Supported Loving network for professionals run by Choice Support (see the Resources section).

In my experience, most poorly managed situations in regards to masturbation occur when someone is trying to manage a situation on their own – they are being a lone wolf. If you have no one to check in with it can be easy to make basic errors, and poor practice and personal values can emerge, putting the client and yourself at risk. Sharing the workload with others can root out poor practice, and you also have shared the responsibility in case an unforeseen or challenging situation does arise in the future.

As well as keeping you safe, sharing practice (while maintaining confidentiality, of course) will ensure that your delivery is refreshed and supported.

SUMMARY

- Create a safe space.
- Undertake a needs assessment to check knowledge.
- Always start with the basics; try not to make assumptions.
- Be a positive role model.
- Check in often with learners' comfort, learning and gaps in knowledge and understanding.
- Share the workload; seek support from those around you.

Chapter 14

Masturbation Education Activities

This chapter contains some of the activities that I use for masturbation education. They are tried and tested and help explore some of the day-to-day and wider issues with masturbation and personal behaviour. Different activities will be effective for different people, so don't forget your needs assessment as discussed in the previous chapter. Most of these activities can be adapted by swapping text for visual images or for oral information, and the activities can either be condensed to focus on the most important issues for the people you are delivering to or expanded on depending on situations that may arise in your organization.

At the end of the book there is a list of suggested resources and where to find them. These are for parents and professionals. There are also some resources that people with learning disabilities can use on their own to explore masturbation.

Often people won't have much of a budget for buying resources but don't worry: it is easy to make your own activities and resources, and homemade resources can often meet the need of the person with learning disabilities much better as they are made just for them rather than being a one-size-fits-all approach.

A word about anatomic models

Condom demonstrators and sex toys can be used as substitutes for penises and vulvas when delivering masturbation education. Alternatively, you can make your own models using craft dough or air-drying clay. Using clay in an educational session about sexual and reproductive anatomy will help teach people about the function and correct names of body parts. They can then be used over clothes to explore masturbation in more depth.

The Sexual Offences Act 2003 makes it clear that engaging people with a mental disorder in sexual activity is illegal, which is why we never teach masturbation on someone's body directly or teach them with a hand-over-hand method on their own penis or vulva. Clear boundaries need to be set out for each professional and person with learning disabilities.

If someone is not making enough associations of how to masturbate effectively when shown over clothes then do not be tempted to show them directly on their bodies. Do not touch their penis or vulva unless performing the intimate care within their care plan. Do not place your hands over theirs or give them instructions while they are actively masturbating. This crosses a professional and legal boundary and you place yourself at risk of disciplinary action and prosecution.

The intentional sexual touching of a person with a mental disorder (for example, learning disability) is illegal under the Sexual Offences Act 2003.

Section 38, Care workers: sexual activity with a person
with a mental disorder –
A person (A) commits an offence if:

a. they intentionally touch another person (B)
b. the touching is sexual
c. B has a mental disorder.

Discussion and group activities
Masturbation brainstorm
Used and adapted with permission from *Jiwsi*[1] – *A Pick 'n'
Mix of Sex and Relationships Education Activities* by Mel Gadd
and Jo Hinchliffe (FPA, 2007).

Masturbation is often seen as a taboo subject, something that
is assumed that everyone does but no one talks about. Often
young people feel that there is something wrong with them if
they masturbate. This exercise is to prompt discussion about
this subject.

Aims/purpose

- Explore what we mean by masturbation and the
  different words to describe it.
- Clarify meanings of words associated with
  masturbation.
- Explore any difference in language when referring to
  men and women masturbating.

Explanation
Remind the participants not to disclose any personal
information during this activity.

---

1   Jiwsi is a Welsh/English hybrid word for 'Juicy', it is the name of the RSE project
    that this work is based on, and was chosen by the young people we work with.

93

Before the exercise, prepare two pieces of flipchart paper with the headings 'Male masturbation' and 'Female masturbation', or 'Penis masturbation' and 'Vulva masturbation'.

Split the group into two smaller groups. Give each small group one of the prepared flipchart sheets and ask them to list all the terms they know for male/penis masturbation and female/vulva masturbation.

When they have finished, ask them to come back together as a large group and read out their answers. Discuss the meanings as a whole group and clarify any terms that have not been understood.

The facilitator can ask:

- Were there any differences between male/penis and female/vulva terms? If so, what?
- Was it difficult or easy to do this activity?

Adaptations
For a non-literate group, run a discussion without using the flipchart paper.

Masturbation myths and taboos
Used and adapted with permission from *Jiwsi – A Pick 'n' Mix of Sex and Relationships Education Activities* by Mel Gadd and Jo Hinchliffe (FPA, 2007).

As discussed in the 'Masturbation brainstorm' exercise, masturbation is often seen as a taboo subject. This exercise is to prompt discussion around masturbation, enabling an exploration of the myths and taboos surrounding the topic.

Aims/purpose

- Discuss values and feelings about masturbation in an environment that is distanced from the participants' personal lives.

Adaptations
For a non-literate group, the facilitator can read out the cards.

Explanation
Remind the participants not to disclose any personal information during this activity.

The group sits in a circle. Place the 'Agree' and 'Disagree' title cards at opposite sides of the room or at each end of a table.

Place the discussion cards face down in the middle of the participants.

Ask them, one at a time, to pick up a card, read out the statement and place it at some point between the two cards that reflects how strongly they agree or disagree with the statement. They then state the reasons why they placed it at this point. Once the participant has had the opportunity to give their reasons, the rest of the group can discuss it and move the card if agreed.

The facilitator can ask:

- How easy or difficult is it to talk about masturbation?
- Where would it be appropriate/inappropriate to masturbate?

Agree	Disagree
Most people are happy to talk about masturbation.	Masturbation can stop you having babies in the future.
Masturbation is harmless.	You need to watch porn to masturbate.

People should be free to make their own decisions about masturbation.	You can masturbate in a public toilet.
Your partner should be the only one to give you sexual pleasure.	You should only use your hands to masturbate.
Sex toys are for sexually confident people.	You can't catch sexually transmitted infections if you masturbate on your own.
It is okay to masturbate in front of your sexual partner.	Everybody masturbates.
Masturbation can help you learn about your body.	Not masturbating is normal.
People only masturbate when they haven't got a sexual partner.	Masturbation can make you go blind.
Masturbation makes the palms of your hands go hairy.	Only teenage boys masturbate.
It is embarrassing to talk about masturbating with your partner.	Masturbation is normal.
Masturbation is a private activity.	
Women don't masturbate.	Masturbating can get you into trouble.
We all know the rules about masturbation.	Masturbation is illegal.
You shouldn't masturbate before the age of consent.	You should keep masturbation secret.

The following card statements would definitely go at the 'Agree' end of the continuum:

Masturbation can help you learn about your body
Before you even think about having sex with another person, masturbation can help you have a good understanding of how your own body works, what feels good and what turns you on.

Masturbation is normal
Masturbation is completely normal and okay for anyone to do – despite what some people might tell you.

Not masturbating is normal
Not masturbating is completely normal and okay for anyone to do – despite what some people might tell you.

You can't catch sexually transmitted infections if you masturbate on your own
If you masturbate on your own there is no risk of catching or passing on a sexually transmitted infection. However, if you masturbate with someone else (touching each other's genitals), there may be a risk of getting or passing on a sexually transmitted infection if you, or they, already have an infection. This is because infections can be spread by transferring infected semen or vaginal fluid on the fingers or genital area even if vaginal, anal or oral sex doesn't take place.

People should be free to make their own decisions about masturbation
It is your right to make your own decisions about masturbation.

The following cards would definitely go at the *'Disagree'* end of the continuum:

People only masturbate when they haven't got a sexual partner
People masturbate for lots of different reasons – when they're on their own, in a relationship and/or with their partner, even when the partnered sex they are having is totally satisfying.

Masturbation is illegal
Masturbation is legal if done in a private place.

You shouldn't masturbate before the age of consent
The age of consent only applies to partnered sexual activity. There is no minimum age for masturbation.

Women don't masturbate
It is normal for women to masturbate.

You should only use your hands to masturbate
People use different things to masturbate with.

Sex toys are for sexually confident people
Different people enjoy using sex toys.

Your partner should be the only one to give you sexual pleasure
You have the right to give yourself sexual pleasure, either from masturbating or from partnered sexual activity.

Everybody masturbates
People make different choices about masturbation and it is both normal to masturbate and normal not to masturbate.

Only teenage boys masturbate
People of all ages masturbate.

Masturbation can stop you having babies in the future
Masturbating doesn't make you infertile.

You need to watch porn to masturbate
You don't need to watch porn to masturbate.

You can masturbate in public toilets
No, you can't. Masturbating in public toilets is illegal.

Masturbation can make you go blind
This is a myth. Masturbating doesn't make you go blind.

Masturbation makes the palms of your hands go hairy
This is a myth. Masturbating doesn't make the palms of your hands go hairy.

The following cards wouldn't necessarily go at the *'Agree'* or *'Disagree'* end of the continuum and should instead generate wider discussion:

Masturbation is a private activity
People can masturbate on their own or with a consenting sexual partner (mutual masturbation).

Most people are happy to talk about masturbation
This will depend on you and who you're talking with. People have different boundaries with different people, for example with your friend, with your sexual partner or with your parents. Some people are uncomfortable about talking about sexual activities with anyone.

You should keep masturbation secret
This will depend on you and who you're talking with. Some people prefer to keep masturbation as a personal and private activity, and some people are happy to talk about it.

It is okay to masturbate in front of your sexual partner
This will depend on what you both consent to doing together.

It is embarrassing to talk about masturbating with your partner
This will depend on both you and your partner.

Masturbating can get you into trouble
It is legal for you to masturbate appropriately in a private place. If you masturbate in a public place you could get into trouble.

We all know the rules about masturbation
This will depend on whether you've been told them or not. Some people will know the legal and social rules around masturbation and some people won't.

Masturbation is harmless
This will depend on the situation. Masturbating on your own in a private place is usually harmless; In contrast:

- If you masturbate in a public place you could get into trouble.
- If you masturbate with something unsuitable you could hurt yourself.
- If you masturbate with someone else (touching each other's genitals), there may be a risk of getting or passing on a sexually transmitted infection, if you or they have an infection. This is because infections can be spread by transferring infected semen or vaginal fluid on the fingers or genital area even if vaginal, anal or oral sex doesn't take place.

Public and private

Used and adapted with permission from *Jiwsi – A Pick 'n' Mix of Sex and Relationships Education Activities* by Mel Gadd and Jo Hinchliffe (FPA, 2007).

Resources needed

- Two cards with 'Public' and 'Private' written on them.
- A collection of photographs of public and private places, including a bedroom with one bed, a bedroom with two beds, a bathroom and a toilet.
- A collection of drawings of people taking part in different activities, including people chatting, people hugging, a male and female in underwear, a male and female naked, a male masturbating and a female masturbating.

The number of pictures used can vary according to the needs and abilities of the group – 15 place pictures and 10 activity pictures should be adequate for most groups.

These pictures are readily available in resources such as Picture Yourself (see the Resources section). Facilitators can also collect their own images.

Although we have used the term 'discussion', when working with largely non-verbal groups these discussions are more likely to mean an explanation by the facilitator using whatever communication methods are necessary, for example Makaton, Boardmaker or other visual aids.

Aims/purpose

- Identify and distinguish between pictures of public places and pictures of private places.
- Decide which activities would be appropriate or inappropriate in a public or private place.

Explanation

Discuss with the participants the terms 'public' and 'private'.

Public places are places where more than one person

can be at any time and we have less control over how many people can be there.

Private places are places where one person, or more than one person, can go where they will not be disturbed by others and where they have more control over how many people can be there.

Lay out the two 'Public' and 'Private' cards at opposite ends of the workspace (this could be a table or the floor but should be within the reach of participants).

Explain that each participant will be given a photograph of a place and that in turn they have to show their photograph to the group, communicate what they think the photograph is, decide whether it is a public place or a private place, and then place it near the correct card.

You should go first to provide an example.

The group can then discuss the picture and may wish to change where it lies between public and private. This may result in pictures being placed in the middle of the cards, as some places can be both public and private at different times.

It is usual that by the end of this section there are a lot more pictures identified as public than private.

Next, show the participants the drawings one at a time, describing the activity taking place.

It may be useful to explain what is on each card before showing it to the group, particularly for the more explicit images.

If you choose to show pictures of people masturbating or having sex, then you must decide whether the group will need to do some work to understand these areas prior to this exercise.

As you describe and show each activity card, the participants have to decide whether the activity would be acceptable in a public or a private space. Use prompts; for example when holding up a picture of somebody naked, ask, 'Would this be okay in the supermarket?' (and hold the card over a photo of the supermarket). Hopefully, the answer will be 'No'.

Eventually each activity card should be placed next to or over a photo of where the activity would be acceptable.

As activities are assigned to private places, discuss with participants how private places can be made even more private. For example, participants may decide that masturbating is something that could be done in a bedroom. You can then explore this area by asking the group how they could make a bedroom more private, for example by shutting the door and curtains and then masturbating while covered by the bedclothes.

You should also point out activities that would be illegal in public places and explain that this may lead to getting into trouble with the police.

Adaptations
For less verbal groups, you could use pictures of green ticks and red crosses for participants to indicate if something is acceptable or unacceptable.

My penis social story
Activity designed by Corrina Williams, Cwmni Addysg Rhyw –
Sex Education Company, and used with permission.

Before the session – print or copy out each statement onto paper or card and cut them out so the statements can be mixed up.

During the session – ask the participant to order the cards into a sequence that creates a story or narrative. Discuss each step.

I have a penis.

I keep my penis clean by washing in the bath or shower regularly.

My penis should not be sore or itchy. If my penis is sore or itchy, I need to tell a parent or carer about it.

Now that I have grown up, my penis has changed. It has hair around it and has become bigger. I also get erections.

Erections mean that my penis sometimes becomes bigger and harder and stands up or sticks out.

It is normal to get erections and they can go away on their own.

I might get erections for lots of reasons but having an erection is a private thing. If I get an erection in school I can pull my jumper down to hide it or sit at the table until it goes away. It is never okay to rub my penis in school.

If I am in a private place at home, it can feel nice to rub and touch my penis. Rubbing and touching my penis might give me an erection.

Rubbing and touching my penis on purpose for sexual feelings is called masturbation.

Masturbation is normal and lots of people do it, but only in a private place (do we ever see other people masturbating?).

If I masturbate at home, in a private place, I can enjoy all the good feelings without getting into trouble.

Masturbating shouldn't make my penis feel sore. If

masturbating does make my penis feel sore, I need to speak to a parent or carer.

Sometimes if I have been very excited while masturbating, some white sticky fluid will come out of the end of my penis. This is called ejaculation and this is normal. I will need to clean this up with a tissue, put the tissue in the bin or toilet, and then wash my hands.

My vulva social story

Adapted from 'My penis social story' activity designed by Corrina Williams, Cwmni Addysg Rhyw – Sex Education Company, and used with permission.

Before the session – print or copy out each statement onto paper or card and cut them out so the statements can be mixed up.

During the session – ask the participant/s to order the cards into a sequence that creates a story or narrative. Discuss each step.

I have a vulva.

I keep my vulva clean by washing the outside of my vulva in the bath or shower regularly.

I don't use soap or deodorant inside my vagina as that can make it irritated or sore.

My vulva and vagina should not be sore or itchy. If my vulva or vagina is sore or itchy, I need to tell a parent or carer about it.

Now that I have grown up, my vulva has changed. It has hair around it and I also get discharge coming from my vagina.

Discharge is the wetness that comes out of my vagina and helps keep my vagina and vulva healthy.

If I am in a private place at home, it can feel nice to rub and touch my vulva and clitoris.

Rubbing and touching my vulva on purpose for sexual feelings is called masturbation.

Masturbation is normal and lots of people do it, but only in a private place (do we ever see other people masturbating?).

If I masturbate at home, in a private place, I can enjoy all the good feelings without getting into trouble.

Masturbating shouldn't make my vulva feel sore. If masturbating does make my vulva feel sore, I need to speak to a parent or carer.

Sometimes if I have been very excited while masturbating, more wetness than normal will come out of my vagina. This is normal. I can clean this up with a tissue, put the tissue in the bin or toilet, and then wash my hands.

Chapter 15

Parents and Professionals – Working Together

Professionals – working with parents, carers and people with parental responsibility

Parents, carers and other family members are the biggest assets a professional has when working with young people and adults with learning disabilities. But, let's be honest, a minority of parents/carers can also be the biggest stumbling block or gatekeepers in blocking work regarding sex, relationships and masturbation.

Most parents/carers haven't had training in how to bring up a child with learning disabilities and also cope with their emerging sexuality. They have to learn on the job. It is hard enough to parent a teenager without learning disabilities, who will pick up on the social cues about keeping masturbation private and who will (it is hoped) receive sex education appropriate to their age and developmental ability at their mainstream school. Most parents/carers of a child with learning disabilities are parenting and managing emerging sexuality with the main aim of minimizing harm to their child. While a primarily protective approach is usually right and necessary, it is important that this does not negatively impact on someone's rights to be sexual if they so choose.

Remember, when someone tries to stop sexual behaviour it is usually done with the intention of protecting the person or other people around them. Ideally, we can channel that force for good into other ways of protecting the person with learning disabilities and the people around them by enabling them to masturbate in private should they so wish. Most parents/carers don't want to stop someone masturbating appropriately; they just want to ensure their child is safe from harm.

As professionals, part of our work should be to support an individual with learning disabilities to appropriately learn about and engage in masturbation if they choose to, and everything we do should comply with current law and good practice guidance.

Not all of the people we support have a family who is involved with them; some have social workers and other people who support them. When we refer to parents/carers we are talking about whoever holds parental responsibility for a young person or whoever offers them the key support within their lives.

Parents/carers may experience anxiety around issues concerning masturbation and their child (even when their child is over 16 or an adult). It can be very difficult for some parents/carers to view their child as a sexual being, particularly when the child is vulnerable. We must acknowledge this and help family members through this process.

If we use sexual behaviour plans (see the chapter on sexual behaviour and sex education care plans) they should be available for parents and carers who have parental responsibility, and we should consult with them as appropriate because we will need to consider a consistent approach at school, college and work/volunteer placements, and in a day centre, residential settings and at home.

Parents – working with professionals

The professionals who work with us are the biggest assets we have when parenting our young people and adults with learning disabilities. But, let's be honest: a minority of professionals can also be the biggest stumbling blocks or gate-shutters in obstructing work around sex, relationships and masturbation.

Yes, this cuts both ways. People, parents, professionals – we can be enabling and proactive of people's right to masturbate but we can also block it, and sometimes we get things wrong.

If you are a parent, carer or family member working to support someone in your life to masturbate safely and effectively then carry on doing the amazing work you are doing (I know you are not getting paid to do it but I still say it is work – hard work). Parents and carers can be the best sex educators in someone's life, whether they have a learning disability or not. Communicating openly about growing up, relationships, sex and masturbation from an early age means that most issues can be dealt with before they balloon into big problems.

Common questions parents ask

Is it okay to provide a place for someone to masturbate in?
Yes, as long as it is a private place where the person with a learning disability lives or stays, such as a bedroom, and it is clearly understood why this is a private place.

Is it okay to provide lubricant?
Yes, lubricant is simply a friction-reducing substance. There

is no minimum age limit on using lubricant for personal activities. Water- and oil-based lubricants are widely available at pharmacies and supermarkets, usually near the condoms. Ensure that the lubricant used doesn't irritate the sensitive parts of the body, and suggest different types if it does.

Is it okay to provide a sex toy to a person with learning disabilities?
Sex toys are discussed further in the chapter on sex toys, but there is no legal minimum age for owning and using a sex toy as they are legally defined as novelty items. If a person with a learning disability wants to try a sex toy and can participate in choosing one, then it is okay to provide them with it. If you think someone would find a sex toy beneficial, for example to prevent soreness or injury, then it would be reasonable to provide them with one to try. However, if they have not expressed a desire to try a sex toy and there is no harm-reducing reason to use it, then don't suddenly provide one. You could initiate a conversation about sex toys and take it from there but always be led by the personal choice of the person.

How do you explain to a child/young person/adult who struggles to understand?
As their parent, you will have the best knowledge of what your child does and doesn't understand. Explore with them what they already know and understand, using straightforward language/visual images/Makaton. If your child has little or no understanding of masturbation then you have the opportunity to take control of the topic and give clear guidance on what it is and that, although completely normal, it is a private activity. Explain where it is okay to do it too. Sometimes working from this starting point is easier than trying to correct misunderstandings and false information.

How do you explain to someone who is non-verbal?
How do we explain anything to someone who is non-verbal?
We use visual images and repetition. Explaining masturbation
is the same as explaining toilet hygiene or road safety; we
give clear visual learning cues and check in regularly with
someone's understanding.

Is it okay to tell a child that masturbation feels pleasurable?
Yes, it is, but this message should ideally be part of wider
relationships and sex education. We should also include the
information that while masturbation is a normal thing to do,
it isn't something that everybody does so they can choose
themselves if they want to masturbate or not. And, of course,
it should only be done in private.

What age is the right age to teach about masturbation?
Masturbation isn't really a standalone topic. Masturbation
education should be included within body awareness, public
and private behaviour and social and legal rules, all of which
are taught from a very early age whether we are aware of
it or not. It is normal to teach preschool children not to
touch their genitals in public and this can be part of early
masturbation education (i.e. it's okay to touch your own bits
in private but not in public).

How do I have a conversation about masturbation?
Just do it. It gets easier with practice, I promise! There is more
information about how to approach masturbation education
in the chapter on talking about masturbation.

They can't seem to climax. What can I do?
This can be very frustrating for someone who wants to
experience an orgasm. I discuss the reasons for not climaxing
in the chapter on how to masturbate. A simple solution can
be to provide sufficient private time and some water-based

lubricant which is commonly available from pharmacies and supermarkets. This can be effective for both males and females.

I am used to providing intimate care for my child. Can I help them masturbate?
Legally you can't physically help your child to masturbate. You can place their hands on their own private parts then give then some privacy or you can provide a sex toy (as discussed earlier) and give them some privacy. Although helping someone to masturbate can seem a small step to take if you are doing everything else for your child, the law makes it very clear that masturbating your child is illegal.

My child wears incontinence pads. What can I do in this situation?
Incontinence pads can severely impede someone's opportunity to explore their own genitals and masturbate if they want to. It is good practice to provide your child with some time each day without a pad so they can touch themselves if they want to. Maybe in the bath (if safe to do so) or when changing from or into nightwear.

My child has to be under constant supervision. How do I give them private time but still keep them safe?
If your child needs constant supervision, explore how you can introduce some privacy into their life. Maybe they could have some time where they are supervised from outside the room by occasional checks through a partially open door?

My child has a physical impairment that means they can't use their hands to masturbate. What can they do?
There are a range of resources and sex toys available for people who have physical impairments which mean they can't use their hands to masturbate. With their consent,

explore what sort of aid they would like to try. It has to be something they could use independently as it is illegal for a parent to physically use an aid or sex toy on their child to masturbate them. In the next chapter, we explore sex toys more fully.

Chapter 16

Sex Toys, Fetish Items, Pornography, Sexting and Sex Workers

Sex toys

We use objects for a variety of tasks in our lives. We sit on chairs or sleep in beds instead of on the floor; we use toothbrushes to clean our teeth; and we can use cutlery or chopsticks instead of our fingers when eating. Sex toys are objects that can help us experience sexual pleasure in an easier or different way from just using our hands.

It may come as a surprise to some people but there is no legal minimum (or maximum) age limit to purchasing sex toys and using them for solo masturbation. In the UK, they are legally defined as novelty items so are not subject to any minimum age restrictions. However, most retailers will set their own age restrictions due to the toys being used for sexual activities. Historically if you wanted to buy a sex toy you would have to visit a sex shop or buy it by mail order. As sex shops often also sell pornographic materials, they usually have a minimum age of 18 for customers. Nevertheless, more and more retailers are starting to offer sex toys as part of their range of personal wellness products, and sex toys are no longer only sold in sex shops. You can easily find sex toys on shelves in high street stores or large supermarkets, and they are also widely available online. Retailers such as high street pharmacies or online retailers will permit purchase if you are over the legal age of consent for sex: 16 years old. However, age limits will be different for each retailer so it is best not to make any assumptions before you buy.

All the usual legal and social rules about masturbation and sexual activity will still apply if you are using sex toys.

There are many different kinds of sex toys, designed for different body parts, needs and purposes. Some sex toys look like people's penises, vulvas and anuses, while others look like bath toys or more abstract objects. Some sex toys are designed to be inserted inside a vagina or anus, while others are designed to stimulate the body externally.

Broadly sex toys fall into the following categories:

- *Dildo*: These are toys that are designed to be inserted into a vagina and/or anus. They come in different sizes and shapes and are made of different materials such as plastic, rubber and glass.
- *Butt plugs*: Whereas dildos are usually designed to be moved in and out of a vagina or anus, butt plugs are designed to stay inserted to give a full sensation to the rectum. Butt plugs have flared ends so can't get stuck inside the rectum. It is important to only insert sex toys with flared ends into an anus as it is easy for 'unflared' sex toys to travel too far inside the rectum and then medical help may be needed to get them out.
- *Vibrators*: As the name indicates, these toys vibrate and, depending on the type, can be used to stimulate the body internally (vagina/anus) and/or externally (vulva/clitoris/penis/testicles/anus). As well as stimulating genitals, they can be used to massage other parts of the body as preferred.

- *Clitoral/prostate stimulators*: These can range from vibrators to ridged toys and are designed to specifically stimulate the clitoris or prostate. A clitoris has 8000 nerve endings and many people need direct clitoral stimulation rather than vaginal stimulation to achieve orgasm.

Supporting someone to buy a sex toy

If a client is old enough (depending on the source of purchase, this will be different ages) and has the capacity to choose equipment then you can support them to exercise their choice to buy and use a sex toy. Education may need to be put in place on how to look after the equipment, keep the equipment private, keep it clean, charge it or change batteries, and ask for help if the device stops working or breaks.

Supporting someone to use a sex toy

It is reasonable to show a person with learning disabilities how to use a sex toy on a model, a doll or a puppet or against their hand. However, it is never okay to use the sex toy on the person's body for their (or your) sexual gratification.

If someone cannot use a sex toy for themselves but they have expressed that they'd like to use one there are options in the form of sex toys with remote switches or vibrating pads where you can position the person with a sex toy then leave the room in order for them to use it privately. Sometimes a person is not able to express a preference about using a sex toy; it can be tempting to provide them with one, thinking it is in their best interests, but this needs to be approached with care. If they can't express a preference, how do you know that providing them with a toy is in their best interests? Maybe there are obvious clues such as them trying to use an unsuitable object and so exchanging it with a toy may prevent harm. Maybe once they've tried a toy they will be happier. I would always say that someone needs to have control or choice over their own sexual experience, but if there is a team consensus that providing a sex toy would reduce harm then the reasoning and decision behind introducing a sex toy should be included in their individual care or sexual behaviour plan.

SUMMARY

- Sex toys have no minimum legal age limit for purchase and use.
- They need to be kept clean.
- They need to be kept private.
- Sex toys need to be thrown away and replaced when they break or wear out.

Fetish items

As people with learning disabilities may not have the cognitive ability or social access to form socially normative sexual stimulants, it is common for them to associate other items with sexual arousal, such as fabrics, personal care items, pets or household objects.

Try to use common sense to separate your own values around masturbation and sex from the personal preferences of a person with learning disabilities. Most fetishes are a normal expression of sexual preference; think about all the fetishes that have become part of mainstream sexual culture such as leather, feathers, food, shoes and bondage gear!

Try not to make assumptions about why a client is using a particular item; for example, using nappies to masturbate into may be because the nappy represents a hygiene item for body fluids rather than representing a sexual interest in children. However, using pets as fetish items is not legal under the Sexual Offences Act 2003, so should be stopped.

If the fetish item is unsuitable, such as a pet or an unsafe object, explore why the client has identified it as a fetish item and seek possible safe and legal alternatives, such as a piece of fake fur fabric or a sex toy.

Fetish item box

As many fetish items are everyday objects, it can be confusing as to which objects are acceptable to masturbate with. Also it can be tempting to stop someone using fetish objects to masturbate with altogether, out of fear of harm or inappropriate behaviour. However, someone without learning disabilities can masturbate with the objects they choose as they (usually) have some understanding of how to keep the behaviour private and how to keep themselves safe. We need to support people with learning disabilities to be able to exercise these same rights where possible.

Consider how you could facilitate the use of a fetish item in a safe way that doesn't negatively impact on other people. If a person likes using common household objects, for example wearing rubber washing-up gloves when masturbating, then provide some of those items in a distinctive colour or with a label with the person's name on. Provide them with a box so they can keep the objects separate from the rest of the household objects. The box can be kept close to their bed, or close to the place where they choose to masturbate in their private room. Set clear boundaries about which objects are okay to be used for sexual activity and which are not.

As with any other materials used for sexual activities, fetish objects should only be used in private and they should be kept clean.

Sai masturbates in private but he likes to have his pet dog in his room as he adores him. His family suspects that he is masturbating onto the dog's fur. With support from the local learning disability team he is provided with some education about what is appropriate when masturbating and what is not. The family set a rule that the dog is not allowed in Sai's room when he is masturbating. However, as the feel of the dog's fur is probably an arousal aid, he is provided with some fun fur to touch and he is taught how to keep it private and to put it in the washing machine after use.

SUMMARY

- Label the items.
- Store the items separately.
- Educate the individual on how to keep the items clean.
- Know what to do if the item breaks or is worn out.

Pornography

Pornography includes any visual materials that contain sexually explicit descriptions and/or visual images that are designed to sexually stimulate or arouse the person looking at them. In the UK, it is legal to buy legal pornography when you are 18 years old or over.

Illegal pornography in the UK includes depictions of: non-consensual sexual activity; sexual activity that threatens a person's life; sexual activity which results, or is likely to result, in serious injury to a person's genitals, anus or breasts; sexual activity involving people who are under 18 or who are depicted to be under 18 (including cartoon images); and sexual activities involving animals or dead people.

If a client is 18 or over and has the capacity to choose legal pornography then (within your workplace policy) you can support them to exercise their choice. It is reasonable to give a client who is 18 or over information on how to access legal pornography and how to use the internet safely if they express an interest in it.

However, do not provide a client with pornographic material such as online content or a magazine because you think they would enjoy it. If a person with a learning disability lacks capacity to make the choice to view pornography then showing them pornography could be considered illegal. Also, your tastes, perceptions and assumptions of sexual stimulants will be different to theirs. Most mainstream lads/girls' mags and porn follow a fairly binary, heterosexual script. By choosing and providing materials you are probably drawing from your own assumptions and sexual preferences rather than theirs.

Unless they are living independently, a person with learning disabilities may need to negotiate access to view internet pornography as they could be prevented from doing so by the parents/carers and the home owner who will be paying the internet bill and may own the devices on which the person with learning disabilities wants to access pornography. This may impact on the other users of the device and it may not be appropriate to share devices if there are young people under 18 or other vulnerable people in the household. If someone wants to use pornography, it is recommended that they have a device for their sole use and know how to close website pages after they have looked at them.

If the person with learning disabilities is living in shared accommodation it is also crucial that their use of pornography doesn't impact on the other people who live with them. Use of the internet can be a rights issue, as many people with learning disabilities find their internet access blocked or impeded by the gatekeepers within their lives. Access to online information, services, education, entertainment, friendships and relationships is a right that everyone should be able to enjoy. If the worry is that someone will be at risk due to their online access then the solution should always be education and support first rather than blocking access completely.

Most people who don't have a learning disability can reasonably expect to be able to enjoy legal pornography privately if they choose to do so. A person with a learning disability may need support to exercise this choice. Whatever your personal feelings about pornography are it is important to remember that if your client is over 18 and has the capacity to choose and access legal pornography then that is their choice and their right to do so.

A pornography actor has the right to be fairly paid for their work. You may have a range of values and feelings about pornography but that does not mean that we should exploit actors' rights when they are providing a paid service. Free pornography is paid for by advertising and often provides quantity rather than quality of porn. If you are going to enjoy pornography then it is worth considering paying for it as it is usually more ethical to pay for it rather than to only access free pornography.

Sexting

Sexting is when individuals use digital technology such as mobile phones or computers to send and receive self-generated sexual or naked images to and from each other, for example sending someone a naked selfie. Sexting is also known as 'sending nudes'. Sexting is legal if all the people engaged in it are 18 or over and are fully consenting to creating, sending and receiving the sexual images. If any of the parties are under 18, even if they are 16 (and therefore over the age of consent) and have taken a picture of themselves, the sexting is illegal and is classed as distributing an illegal photograph of a child. If the people involved are over 18 but don't consent to the image being created and shared then that is illegal and could be classed as a revenge pornography offence (disclosing private sexual photographs and films with intent to cause distress).

SUMMARY

- Although the UK age of consent for sex is 16, you need to be an adult and 18 or over to legally access and use pornography.
- Some pornography is illegal for everyone.
- If a person with a learning disability has the capacity to choose and access legal pornography then you can support them to do so.

Sex workers

If you are over 18 years of age and have the capacity to consent to sexual activity, and do so freely, then selling or buying sex is not illegal in itself. However, there are offences around sex work (prostitution) which make paying for sex somewhat complex and potentially illegal, especially if any of the parties involved are not free to make their own choices or are not fully understanding of the issues involved and not freely consenting.

Section 39 of the Sexual Offences Act 2003 prohibits care workers from 'causing' or 'inciting' someone with a 'mental disorder' to engage in sexual activity. If someone we support is old enough and has the capacity, independence and means to employ a sex worker, we can support them in the same way as we would any other adult in regards to their sexual health by providing them with the same education and support as they would get for any other sexual relationship.

However, staff can't take any action to facilitate or engage a sex worker for someone with a learning disability. It is also illegal to provide help in the delivery of sex services, so knowingly allowing premises for sex work to take place could be considered illegal.

Sometimes we hear of parents or carers who wish to engage a sex worker for their adult child (under 18 it is illegal for both worker and client), thinking it would be in their best interests to have sex with someone within their control rather than wait for a sexual relationship to start in another way. But, if the person with learning disabilities doesn't fully understand and consent to the engagement of a sex worker, this could be considered illegal.

Section 31 of the Sexual Offences Act 2003

Causing or inciting a person, with a mental disorder impeding choice, to engage in sexual activity –
A person (A) commits an offence if:

a. they intentionally cause or incite another person (B) to engage in an activity
b. the activity is sexual
c. B is unable to refuse because of or for a reason related to a mental disorder, and
d. A knows or could reasonably be expected to know that B has a mental disorder and that because of it or for a reason related to it B is likely to be unable to refuse.

B is unable to refuse if:

a. they lack the capacity to choose whether to

> agree to engaging in the activity caused or
> incited (whether because they lack sufficient
> understanding of the nature or reasonably
> foreseeable consequences of the activity, or for
> any other reason), or
> b. they are unable to communicate such a choice
> to A.

In relation to solo masturbation, sometimes people
employ sex workers by talking with them on the phone via
commercial sex lines or by communicating with them on the
internet via chatrooms and webcams. Even though this is not
physically touching, the same rules around age (18 and over),
capacity to consent, and giving and receiving consent apply.
It is important that people with learning disabilities who
wish to purchase these services understand the difference
between commercial sex workers and chatting to a boyfriend
or girlfriend via these methods. It is also important to
ensure that the person is clear about what services they are
purchasing, how much they will cost and how to make sure
that all involved in the transaction are not being exploited.
Having an open dialogue about what is being purchased,
what it costs, who is involved, and the spoken/unspoken
contract between the sex worker and the client is important
for everyone's sakes.

I would also add that a sex worker has the right to be
fairly paid for their work. You may have a range of values
and feelings about sex workers but that does not mean that
we should exploit their rights when they are providing a paid
service.

SUMMARY

- Sex work is not illegal.
- You have to be over 18 to provide or purchase sex work.
- Issues around capacity and consent are key, and it is illegal to procure a sex worker for a person with a learning disability on their behalf.

Showing respect for others

A part of our right to enjoy sex toys, fetish items, legal pornography, sex lines and online sexual content is our responsibility to ensure that our use of these materials doesn't impact on other people. Many people with learning disabilities live with other people, whether it is their family or in shared or supported accommodation. It is important that their use of sex toys, fetish items, pornography and sexual materials is kept as private as their masturbation should be.

If someone enjoys accessing pornography online then it would be best if they had a device (laptop, tablet or phone) for their own use. If there is a household computer or laptop that everyone uses (especially children and young people), it is recommended that parental controls and adult content filters are enabled for under-18s and that each user has their own account and private password.

Sex toys, fetish items and visual pornography should be kept in private bedrooms and if someone other than the bedroom owner has access to the room (for personal care, cleaning, collecting laundry and so on), the materials should be kept safely out of sight when not being used. This is especially important if the person shares a bedroom with someone else, such as a sibling.

If using services by phone or online then the user should ensure that they are not being overheard or seen by others.

Chapter 17

Common Situations and Good Practice Responses

Responding to inappropriate masturbation can feel awkward and challenging if done without previous experience, guidance or training. Unfortunately, training on how to respond to masturbation is not routinely available, and many organizations don't include policy guidance on how to respond when staff are faced with inappropriate masturbation.

There is usually no single 'best' way to manage complicated behaviour and this book certainly won't have all the answers for everyone; however, I hope it will explore some of the most common situations and give guidance on a starting point for managing common masturbation-related situations. Before you take action, it may be useful to ask yourself these questions to help you come up with an appropriate response to the situation:

- Does the behaviour result from anything else?
- Is the behaviour legal or illegal?

- Does the person's behaviour negatively impact or harm themselves or anyone else?
- Is the behaviour taking place in public or private?
- How does it make you feel? Do your feelings need to be taken into account?
- How can you best respect the rights of the person and those around them?
- What, if any, action are you going to take?

If the self-touching is for reasons other than an intent to masturbate, then once you have checked that the person is well, you can use distraction techniques to occupy their interest as an initial response. As we explored in the chapter on 'What else could it be?', sometimes the self-touch is not about masturbation and sexual activity. However, if there is an intent to inappropriately masturbate for sexual stimulation, a response with clear boundaries needs to be given.

Many professionals can find it difficult to directly challenge inappropriate masturbation. But, it is behaviour that has to be challenged. Like most things in life, it gets easier with practice!

- Where possible, challenge the person in private, on their own and with respect.
- Use a clear, assertive voice accompanied with clear hand gestures, and visual aids and symbols if needed.
- Look shocked and unimpressed. Do not use humour to lessen embarrassment or laugh it off. The consequences of inappropriate masturbation can have a serious impact on the person themselves and those around them, this message needs to be conveyed.
- Give clear instructions of how or where the behaviour would be okay.

A person with learning disabilities has little or no understanding of public and private places
Example situations

'Zain, stop touching your penis. We do not touch our private parts/penis in the classroom. You can only do that in a private place at home!'

'Eira, stop rubbing your vulva against the desk. We do not rub our private parts/vagina in the classroom. You can only do that in a private place at home!'

It is reasonable to give clear or exaggerated facial expressions, body language and social cues so that people with learning disabilities can learn what response they may receive from people if they engage in public masturbation and what is deemed socially acceptable behaviour. This is in the same vein as the reaction you may give to teach anyone any other safe behaviour; we react strongly in order to impress the importance and gravity of the situation and the weight of the consequences if the behaviour continues unchecked.

It is important also not to use humour or 'laugh off' the behaviour. This is a natural human response when we feel uncomfortable or embarrassed about a situation or when we are trying to lessen someone else's discomfort or put them at ease. The reality is that public masturbation is an uncomfortable and illegal situation, and masking the effects or consequences of inappropriate masturbation can make the behaviour seem more socially acceptable than it actually is.

However, make sure you address the behaviour rather than the person. Do not use words like dirty, naughty or disgusting. Give clear directions as to where the behaviour would be acceptable and, most importantly, clarify that masturbation is normal, legal and pleasurable but you have to be in a private place to engage in it.

You may find it helpful to practise saying useful or key phrases when you are on your own or during an appropriate time such as a staff training or supervision session. Repeat the phrase until you can say it clearly and without embarrassment. Being able to give clear directions with confidence will minimize embarrassment for both you and the person you are talking with.

Keep it quite basic if needed: 'Zain, stop touching your penis.'

Good practice responses

Male (14) gets erections at school and touches his penis under the desk.

- In private, say, 'Stop touching your private parts [*or* penis]. We do not touch our private parts [*or* penis] in the classroom. You can only do that in a private place at home!'
- Check that there is not an underlying or undiagnosed health problem.
- Check whether the person has a private space at home, and if not, suggest he does have one.
- Run a 'public/private' education session with the person and/or with the whole class.
- Deliver a relationships and sex education (RSE) programme to the class.

Female (17) at school rubs her vulva against the corner of the desk.

- In private, say, 'Stop rubbing your private parts [*or* vagina] against the desk. We do not rub our private parts [*or* vagina] in the classroom. You can only do that in a private place at home!'

- Check that there is not an underlying or undiagnosed health problem.
- Check whether the person has a private space at home, and if not, suggest she does have one.
- Run a 'public/private' education session with the person and/or with the whole class.
- Deliver an RSE programme to the class.

At college Noor repeatedly masturbates himself under the table during class. The staff find this embarrassing and do not know how to stop this behaviour. A series of RSE education sessions are delivered to the class by an experienced facilitator. When the masturbation takes place the facilitator clearly says, 'Please don't touch your private parts in class. Wait until you are in your bedroom at home.' The staff gain a 'script' for how to challenge the behaviour and also create a 'public and private places' image wall with pictures of the public places around the school and the pupil's private places at home. They spend ten minutes each day reinforcing the messages about public and private places and, along with a repeated challenge whenever they witness public masturbation, the inappropriate masturbation comes to an end.

Example situation
Male (16) gets sexually frustrated and masturbates in the school toilets.

Using a public toilet (including at school or college), for sexual activities, including masturbation, is illegal (see the chapter on masturbation and the law). This becomes additionally problematic if other children or young people (under-18s) are exposed to the behaviour.

I recommend that you run an educational programme with clear explanations of public and private places and that masturbating at school is not acceptable. Ensure that the student has a private space and time at home in order to masturbate if he chooses to do so. If sexual frustration is affecting behaviour negatively then staff and family should work on teaching other self-soothing or distraction activities to help manage behaviour as alternatives to masturbation at school.

Good practice response

- Ensure that staff know that sexual activity in school toilets is illegal.
- Run a 'public/private' education session with the person with learning disabilities and/or whole class.
- Tell the person, 'The school toilet is not a private place for private activities like masturbating. You can only use the toilets for weeing and pooing, because other people who use the toilets can hear you. You can only masturbate at home in a private place.'
- Check whether the person with learning disabilities has a private space at home, and if not, suggest he does have one.
- Deliver an RSE programme to the class.

Example situation
Female (19) rubs her vulva when watching television in the living room of her family home.

Masturbating in a private home, even in the living room, is not illegal if you are on your own or any person who can see you is consenting. However, masturbating in a shared space could be inappropriate or become illegal if there are non-consenting people present, especially children and/or vulnerable adults.

Run an educational programme with clear explanations of public and private places and that masturbating in a shared space is not acceptable. Ensure that the person has a private space and time in order to masturbate if she chooses to do so. Staff and family should explore other self-soothing or distraction activities to help manage behaviour in public places as alternatives to masturbation.

If a particular television programme, cartoon or film (no matter how innocuous it is thought to be) is observed to get a response of masturbatory behaviour then it would be sensible for the person to watch that material in their bedroom, on their own, so they can enjoy masturbating to it in private. Also avoid the viewing of excitable material in shared spaces.

Good practice response

- Run a 'public/private' education session with the client.
- Encourage the parents to tell the person, 'The living room is not a private place for private activities like masturbating. You can only masturbate in a private place like your bedroom.'
- Check whether the person has a private space at home and suggest she does have one.
- Deliver a 'public/private' education session and RSE programme to her class.

Example situation
Male (15) starts masturbating in the classroom in front of other students and staff. He doesn't stop masturbating when requested to.

Masturbating in public and in front of non-consenting people, especially children, is illegal. In this situation, the primary duty of care is to the other children in the room as they could witness a sexual offence. Treat this as you would any other behaviour that puts children or vulnerable people at risk. Immediately remove the other children from the room and take them to a safe place. Do your best to ensure people cannot witness the masturbation incident by closing the classroom door and window coverings. Place a screen around the person masturbating if necessary. I would not recommend touching the person who is masturbating while they are engaging in sexual behaviour. After the incident, generate an incident report and plan how to minimize the risk of this occurring again. This is a serious situation and should be treated as such. Normalizing masturbation in public gives everyone the wrong messages about public and private sexual behaviour and can increase people's vulnerability to harm and reduce a person's dignity. It can also place them at risk of investigation and prosecution if they then engage in the same behaviour in front of someone who makes a complaint to the police.

Good practice response

- Follow your usual incident procedure.
- Ensure other people, especially children and vulnerable people, are protected from harm.
- Plan how to minimize the incident from occurring again.

Cam was reported for engaging in public masturbation. It transpired that Cam goes outside to masturbate as they think they'd get into trouble if their mum 'caught them' doing it at home. On assessment, it becomes evident that Cam has poor understanding of the legal and social rules around masturbation. Cam receives some needs-based RSE, including information on public and private places, parts of the body, and the rules about masturbating in private, as well as additional sessions on masturbation and the law. Cam's family are very supportive; reassure Cam that they can have 'alone time' in their room and the family will respect Cam's need for privacy. Cam makes a sign for their door so that the family know to knock and wait before coming in. There are no further incidents of inappropriate public masturbation.

A person with learning disabilities shares a bedroom with a sibling
Example situation
Female (16) wants to masturbate but shares a bedroom with a younger sister.

Masturbating in your bedroom is perfectly legal if you are on your own and no one other than a consenting person can see you. However, masturbating in a shared space such as a shared bedroom could be inappropriate or become illegal if there were non-consenting people present or children or people with whom it is not legal to have a sexual relationship, such as a sibling. Sharing a bedroom with someone is a common issue and steps should be taken to ensure that each bedroom user gets some time alone in the room. If this is an issue for a person with learning disabilities then also assume that it is or will become an issue for their sibling.

Good practice response

- Run a 'public/private' education session with the person with learning disabilities.
- Explain to both siblings that they are entitled to some time alone in their bedrooms if they so wish.
- Set rules and a rota with the sisters that allow them both to have alone time in their bedroom.
- Create a sign for the bedroom door that either of the sisters can put up during their sole use of their bedroom.
- Check that this system is working on a regular basis.

Responses for requests for private time in a public environment (school, college, work)
Example situation
Male work placement volunteer (22) requests to use the staff toilet for private time.

Using a public toilet, including a staff toilet, for sexual activities (e.g. masturbation) is illegal. This becomes additionally problematic if other people, especially children or vulnerable adults, may be exposed to this behaviour.

If, in the past, a person with learning disabilities has been allowed to use public toilets to masturbate in it may seem normal for them to assume they can carry on doing this in a new work, education or placement environment. Be clear about what is legal behaviour in this setting and where else self-touch and masturbation can take place in an appropriate way.

Good practice response

- Ensure that staff know that sexual activity in staff toilets is illegal.

- Run a 'public/private' education session with the person.
- Tell the person with learning disabilities, 'The staff toilet is not a private place for private activities like masturbating. You can only use the toilets for weeing and pooing because other people who use the toilets might hear or see you. You can only masturbate at home in a private place.'
- Check whether the person with learning disabilities has a private space at home, and if not, suggest he does have one.
- Deliver an RSE programme if possible.
- Where possible, challenge the person in private.
- Use a strong/strict voice accompanied with clear hand gesture and symbol if needed.
- Look shocked and unimpressed. Do not use humour or laugh it off.
- Give clear instructions: 'This is not a private place for private activities like masturbating. You can only use the toilets for weeing and pooing because other people who use the toilets can hear you. You can only masturbate at home in a private place.'

A person with learning disabilities is unable to 'complete' (orgasm) and/or has chafing and soreness
Example situation
Male (22) in residential accommodation is given private time in his own room but is complaining of genital soreness and feeling frustrated.

Many people with learning disabilities who do not have access to good RSE and educational material about sex and masturbation may find masturbation difficult. For further guidance on this see the chapter on how to masturbate.

Good practice response

- Check that the person's private time is really private and undisturbed. If anyone can enter a room whenever they want then that room is not a private place.
- Check that the length of undisturbed time is sufficient for someone to masturbate if they wish to do so.
- Explore what the person with learning disabilities is really complaining about; check that the genital soreness is not due to illness or a medical condition that needs attention.
- Deliver an RSE programme to the person with learning disabilities.
- Provide water-based lubricant and explain how to use it and how to maintain good personal hygiene.
- After an intervention, arrange a date to check on the issue and see if the soreness and emotional frustration have reduced.
- Explore what else the person with learning disabilities may need to meet their sexual needs.

Sexual response to non-sexually intended touch
Example situation
Male (15) displays behavioural problems, and carer gives him head massages to calm him down. He has started getting noticeable erections during the massages.

- If a carer gives touch that is not intended as sexual which then elicits a sexual response, the carer should discontinue that touch.
- If the carer continues the touch after the sexual

response has been noted then the touch could be perceived as being deliberate and sexual.

- The carer should discontinue the touch immediately.
- The reason for the touch being stopped should be explained to the person with learning disabilities.
- Alternatives to the touch should be explored, and reasons why the touch has changed should be written into the person's care or sexual behaviour plan.
- It is common for young people going through puberty to start becoming sexually aroused by physical touch. This is a normal human response.

It is good practice for a school or organization to explore and question the use of touch in the educational or organizational setting. We know that touching can happen for many different reasons, and some people have visual impairments or other physical impairments that require touch to be a routine part of their education and care. We are sensitive to the fact that most touching (including hugging) happens out of concern for the welfare of the person with learning disabilities or because a long-term bond has built up between the worker and person with learning disabilities, or because the person with learning disabilities initiates the touch. However, this does not mean that touching a person with learning disabilities is the most appropriate way to work with them. Holding a person's hand or arm when there is an identified need to do so is appropriate, but holding their hand when walking because that's what you've always done is not. You would not expect to see a teacher (of either gender) holding a student's hand in a mainstream school or college setting as they walk down a corridor or in a classroom, so the same professional boundaries should apply to learning disability settings.

You can future-proof your care provision for when a child grows into an adult by asking these questions:

- Why are you touching the person with learning disabilities?
- How does this touch benefit the person with learning disabilities?
- What would be the outcome of discontinuing this touch?
- Is this touch appropriate for the lifetime of the person with learning disabilities?
- What happens when they go through puberty?
- Would it be appropriate for a colleague of a different gender to touch them in this way?
- Would it be appropriate for staff to touch the person with learning disabilities in this way in private?
- What are other ways you could use to manage any challenging behaviour?

If you notice a sexual response to touch and then repeat the touch again then you are potentially committing a sexual offence. This may be unavoidable for staff delivering personal care but not for other touching. If you are delivering personal care and notice a sexual response to touch, refer to your intimate care policy.

If staff members routinely touch people with learning disabilities as normal practice in your school or organizational setting it can be challenging to put the spotlight on it. Many professionals feel the touch is done for the benefit of the person with learning disabilities and are uncomfortable questioning their own or others' practice. If it is truly for the benefit of the person with learning disabilities then it is not an issue and can be written into their care or sexual behaviour plan.

Inappropriate non-sexual touching can reduce a person's independence and ability to practise self-reliance and self-soothing behaviour. At best, it can create confusion about social boundaries with friends, professionals and strangers.

At worst, it can make a person more vulnerable to abuse as they will regard being touched by a range of people who are not family or friends as normal, acceptable or even wanted behaviour.

Good practice response

- Educate the carer that head massages are no longer appropriate and why this is. Explain the law relating to sexual touch and adults in a position of trust.
- Explore with the person with learning disabilities, parents and staff other ways in which staff could respond to any behavioural problems.
- Run a 'public/private' education session with the person with learning disabilities and/or the whole class.
- Check whether the person with learning disabilities has a private space at home, and if so, suggest he does have one.
- Deliver an RSE programme to the class.

Sexual responses to non-sexual touch at home

Sometimes people with learning disabilities will respond sexually to non-sexual touch in ways such as rubbing their genitals when being hugged and cuddled by family and friends. This can be a challenging situation for the young person and family and friends alike, as family non-sexual physical touch is valuable and shouldn't be discouraged if possible. We encourage this sexual response to be challenged at onset of early behaviour.

Good practice response

- Where possible challenge the person in private.

- Use a strong, strict voice accompanied with clear hand gesture and symbol if needed.
- Look shocked and unimpressed. Do not use humour or laugh it off.
- Give clear instructions.

'Dewi, stop touching your penis. You do not touch your private parts or penis when you are having a cuddle with me. You can only do that in your private place on your own!'

'Ffion, stop rubbing your vulva against me. You do not rub your private parts or vulva when I'm giving you a cuddle. You can only do that in your bedroom on your own!'

It is reasonable to give clear or exaggerated social cues so that people can learn what is legally and socially acceptable; we react strongly in order to impress the importance and gravity of the situation and the weight of the consequences if the behaviour is not corrected.

However, make sure you address the behaviour rather than the person. Do not use words like 'dirty', 'naughty' or 'disgusting'. Give clear directions as to where the behaviour would be acceptable. Clarify that masturbation is normal and pleasurable but you have to be in a private place to engage in the activity.

Practise saying the phrases when you are on your own or during an appropriate time. Saying it clearly with confidence minimizes embarrassment for you and the young person. Keep it more basic if needed: 'Dewi, stop touching your penis when I cuddle you.'

SUMMARY

- Masturbation is a normal activity.

- Try to separate your personal values from good practice.
- Try to plan for this situation before it happens. Create a policy and adapt it as needed.
- Provide clarity about public and private places and private behaviour.
- Provide appropriate education on growing up, sex and relationships.
- Give clear, unambiguous directions if inappropriate activity takes place.
- Work in partnership with the person with learning disabilities, parents/carers and staff.
- Give consistent, clear messages and repeat often.
- Consider the future long-term needs of the person with learning disabilities, not just the here and now.

Chapter 18

Sexual Behaviour and Sex Education Care Plan

A sexual behaviour care plan focuses on a person's sexual rights and behaviour and sets out clear strategies for staff to follow while being a person-centred response to the individual's needs.

A sexual behaviour care plan is usually developed when a person with learning disabilities displays worrying, problematic or harmful behaviour (to themselves and/or others) . If a person is managing their own private sexual behaviour in a way that doesn't impact on other people they will have no more need for a sexual behaviour care plan than any other person.

A sexual behaviour care plan should be developed by the team around the person with learning disabilities and should include the individual themselves, if possible, and their family. It is not good practice to designate an individual staff member to develop a plan on their own, because that is when personal values, misunderstandings and poor practice can creep in, regarding the rights of the person with learning disabilities and the rules around masturbation.

A sexual behaviour plan can be written in the first person

if a person with learning disabilities has direct input into their plan and it reflects their voice, or they can be written in the third person if it gives information about them.

A sexual behaviour care plan will contain the following key elements:

- An introduction to the person
- An explanation of the person with learning disabilities' sexual behaviour for any staff who haven't worked with the person before
- What education and training the person with learning disabilities has received previously or is undergoing now, and what their levels of understanding are
- What rules there are about the person's behaviour
- What action to take if inappropriate sexual behaviour is displayed so that all the staff and family respond in a consistent and appropriate way
- A risk-assessment section to flag up any safety issues for staff who are working with the person with learning disabilities.

Example care plan
(Adapted with permission from Claire Lightley of Lightley Consulting)

THE SUNSHINE CENTRE FOR PEOPLE WITH LEARNING DISABILITIES

Sexual behaviour and sex education care plan

Name Alex Williams	DOB 18/02/04 Age 15	Written by Claire Lightley
Key worker Ana Smith	Reviewed 31/01/19	Reviewed by Mel Gadd

Growing up

I have been going through puberty for around a year now. I have accepted certain changes to my body such as pubic hair, my voice changing and rapid growth spurts.

My sexual behaviour

I am an adolescent young man and I am currently experiencing erections around female members of staff. I frequently get erections when I am having personal care. I will try to guide staff's hands to my erect penis. My erections are frequent and as far as staff know I do not masturbate in my residential setting. They are not sure why this is but think it might be because I do not know how to.

Sex education

I attend a SEND [special educational needs and disabilities] school every day. I have some relationship and sex education lessons at school. The teachers do not talk about masturbation, and I have not had any education sessions or one-to-one support with this yet.

The law

To support me, staff need to know that the law allows me to be taught about erections and masturbation using explicit but appropriate drawings and videos. Never use pornographic materials to teach about erections or masturbation because this might confuse me and I am under 18 so it is against the law. You must never make direct contact with my genitals while you are teaching me because this is illegal and would be very confusing for me. Any form of sexual activity I engage in needs to take place in my private places; this means in places where other people are not, and I can be by myself.

Where I live

I have private spaces such as my bedroom, which I do not share with anyone, and my bathroom, where the door can be locked. I need to be observed when in the bath but not constantly – a quick glance every minute is sufficient. Staff do not need to be present in the rooms with me at all times. I sleep by myself at night.

I can explore my body in the bedroom or bathroom. These are the only places where it is acceptable to do so because they are the only places where I can be in private.

Sexual behaviour care plan

- When I have an erection in a public place you can take me somewhere private. You can explain that it is okay to have sexual feelings but if I get an erection I need to be in private if I want to touch it. My erection will subside on its own if I do not touch it.
- If I try to guide your hand to my penis when it is erect, you must take your hand away and explain that it is not okay for me to do that to you.
- Please use the correct language for penis, as it will be easier for me to understand.
- If I touch you in a personal place when you are caring for me, please remove my hand and tell me that it is not okay for me to touch you there.
- Keep a record of when I touch staff, who it is and where we are, as this might be useful when we plan some education.

- When I have personal care, when possible rota a male member of staff to do it. I do not get erections when men support me with this.
- If you are supporting me with personal care and I get an erection, please leave the room until I do not have it anymore, and explain what you are doing and make sure I am safe.

Sex education care plan

- Teach me about erections and why I have them.
- Teach me about masturbation, that it feels good and how to do it.
- Teach me about public and private places so I can do this safely.
- Use published resources to do this, and never use pornography.
- Repeat the education and do not stop if I don't understand the first time.
- Think about different ways of teaching, with models, videos or drawings.

Risk assessment for staff

- If I try to guide your hand to my penis when it is erect, you must take your hand away and explain that it is not okay for me to do that to you.
- If I try to touch you in a personal place when you are caring for me, please remove my hand and tell me that it is not okay for me to touch you there.
- Keep a record of when I touch staff, who it is and where we are, as I am not allowed to touch staff inappropriately, and it is important that it is taken seriously.
- When I have personal care, when possible rota a male member of staff to do it.

Chapter 19

Developing a Masturbation Policy

For an organization, school, college or care facility (or even a family) to respond best to masturbation, everyone involved should be working consistently and have the same overall aim and working procedures. This will make it easier for the person with a learning disability to access consistent and correct information and messages from all the people who work with them.

In order to achieve a common purpose, several things need to take place, such as working in partnership with parents, adequate staff training and needs-led RSE, but a good starting point is developing a masturbation policy or a wider relationships and sexuality policy that includes masturbation as a key topic.

If you are a professional, does your workplace have a masturbation or relationships and sex education (RSE) policy? If you are a parent, do the services your child accesses have a policy and, if so, have you been provided with a copy? You should have easy access to all the policies that affect the person you are responsible for.

Developing a policy

The aim of a masturbation policy is to give staff consistent guidance to help them manage issues around masturbation and working with people with learning disabilities. It also aims to protect people with learning disabilities from uninformed and inconsistent practice by staff who are not sure how to deal with some of the issues that might arise when someone in their care masturbates inappropriately or needs support to masturbate.

The starting principles for developing a masturbation policy should be:

- The people we support have the right to be sexual and make informed choices about their sexual behaviour.
- The people we support are entitled to access the help, advice and information they need to express their sexuality within lawful behaviour.
- We recognize that all of the people we support are considered vulnerable (in the eyes of the law) in some way. It is part of our duty of care to achieve a balance between ensuring they can exercise their rights and protecting them and other people around them.
- Staff have the right to receive the guidance and training they need in order to provide the necessary support for people with learning disabilities who wish to masturbate.

Developing a policy can seem really daunting when starting with a blank page but once you break it down into the component parts it will become much more straightforward.

Elements to include

What is this policy about?
Is it a broader relationships and sexuality policy that

incorporates masturbation or is it a standalone masturbation policy?

Who is going to be involved in policy development?
Are you involving people with learning disabilities in policy development? Are you involving families? How can the staff be involved? How are you going to involve all the groups of people in the development of the policy?

Why do we need/want this policy?
What has prompted you to develop policy? What are the gaps in existing policy and why do you believe this issue should have a standalone policy?

What do we want to achieve or prevent?
Is the policy about preventing harm? Or is it about promoting the sexual rights of people with learning disabilities, or (best of all) a combination of both approaches?

How are we going to do this?
What steps are you going to take to achieve what you want to do? These need to be achievable by all the people involved in policy implementation.

Who is going to help us – who is going to be involved?
Identify the key people who are going to support the policy development and actions.

What resources can help us? Forms, reports, resources?
Have a central collection of all the resources and links needed to enact the policy. Refer to and be congruent with any confidentiality, whistleblowing and safeguarding, or vulnerable-people policies.

When are we going to review it?
Give a clear timeframe for implementation and renewal and an identified person or team responsible for this. Policies are developmental pieces of work that change and adapt over time based on experience, learning and emerging good practice. If it gets left on a shelf and isn't regularly renewed, it will go out of date and won't stay relevant.

It is recommended that a masturbation policy includes the following:

- Aim and purpose of the policy
- Rights and rules concerning masturbation
- Working with families
- Good practice responses
- Intimate personal care guidance
- Safeguarding
- Whistleblowing
- Signposting
- Associated policies
- Forms and resources
- Useful organizations.

Adapting other organizations' policies
It is very tempting to adapt another organization's policy by just replacing key information such as the name of organization, key person and so on. However, although a policy from another organization can be a useful starting point, it is important to centre your clients' and organization's needs within your own policy. Having users and staff involved in the policy development helps them to 'own' the policy and be more likely to use it as part of everyday practice.

SUMMARY

- The policy doesn't have to be complicated or long; it should just set out what you are going to do, who with and any safeguards that you have in place for people with learning disabilities, families and staff.
- The policy should have team involvement and not just be down to one person to develop and implement.
- The policy should be a working document that is read and understood by staff and reviewed regularly.

Glossary

Additional learning need (ALN): Refers to children and young people with learning, physical or sensory needs that bring up challenges in learning or education as compared to most children of the same age. ALN replaces the term 'special educational need' in Wales.

Agender: Identifying as having no gender, being gender neutral or not identifying with any binary gender label.

Asexual: Not having a sexual attraction to other people.

Binary (gender): Viewpoint that there are only two genders: male and female.

Biological sex: The assignment of gender based on what reproductive organs are visible at birth.

Bisexual: Sexually attracted to males and females.

Cisgender: Someone whose gender identity and biological sex are the same.

Clitoris: Biological female sexual organ. The clitoris is part of the vulva. The small pea-sized head (glans) of the clitoris is visible in front of the urethra and vagina. Most of the clitoris is an internal structure and it extends around the vaginal wall. The clitoris is very sensitive and touching it can be highly pleasurable.

Cwmni Addysg Rhyw: This is `Sex Education Company' in Welsh. Phonetically it is pronounced `Coo-m-nee Ah-this-g Roo'.

Facilitator: Someone delivering an educational session to an individual or group.

Fetish: Where sexual stimulus or gratification is linked to a particular object or objects.

Gender identity: Identification of a person's gender, as defined by themselves. Their gender identity may or may not align with their biological sex.

Genitals: External human reproductive and sexual organs. This includes the vulva, penis, vagina and testicles.

Heteronormative: A viewpoint that expresses heterosexuality as assumed instead of being one of many possibilities of sexual attraction. Heterosexuality is widely 'accepted' as the default sexual orientation by both print and electronic media, education, law-makers and a range of attitudes expressed by society in general.

Heterosexual: Sexually attracted to the opposite gender.

Homosexual: Sexually attracted to the same gender.

Intellectual disability: Term for learning disability used outside the UK.

Learning disability: Term for intellectual disability used in the UK.

LGBTQ+: Lesbian, gay, bisexual, transgender, queer, plus.

Masturbation: Sexual stimulation of one's own genitals for sexual arousal or sexual pleasure, usually (but not always) to the point of orgasm.

Non-binary: Identity outside the gender binary of male and female.

Normative: Perceived standard of normality.

Orgasm: A pleasurable release of built-up sexual tension resulting in a series of contractions or muscle spasms in the vulva and vagina and penis and testicles. Biological males will usually ejaculate semen when they orgasm.

Pansexual: Attracted to people of all genders and gender identities.

Penis: Biological male's external sexual organ. For urination and ejaculation of semen for reproduction. When the person is sexually aroused, a penis will stiffen and enlarge for a short time. This is called an erection. The penis is very sensitive, and touching it can be highly pleasurable.

Pornography (Porn): Materials containing the explicit description or display of sexual organs or activity, intended to stimulate sexual excitement.

Private: Somewhere no one else can see or hear you.

PSHE: Personal, social and health education.

Public: Somewhere others can see and/or hear you.

RSE: Relationships and sex/sexuality education.

RSHP: Relationships, sexual health and parenthood.

SEND: Special educational needs and disabilities.

SRE: Sex and relationships education.

Testicles: Biological male reproductive glands; testicles make sperm and the hormone testosterone. Two testicles are held within the scrotum and are situated just behind the penis. They are sensitive to touch and temperature.

Transgender: A person who identifies their gender as being different from their biological sex or assigned sex at birth.

Urethra: A tube that connects the bladder to the outside of the vulva or penis for urination (peeing).

Vagina: Biological female sexual body part. The vagina extends from the vulva inside the body to the cervix and uterus. The vagina is for sex, giving birth through and for discharging a monthly period. Vaginal discharge that helps keep the vagina healthy also comes out of the vagina.

Vulva: Biological female sexual body part. The vulva is the name for the external area that includes the clitoris, urethra and vagina.

References

Age of Legal Capacity (Scotland) Act 1991. [online] Available at:
www.legislation.gov.uk/ukpga/1991/50/section/2 [Accessed
21 September 2020].

Bailey, D. (2020). *Breaking Down Gender Stereotypes in Legal
Writing*. Civil Service. [online] Available at: https://civilservice.
blog.gov.uk/2020/01/10/breaking-down-gender-stereotypes-in-
legal-writing [Accessed 14 November 2020].

BAILII.org (2020). *Gillick v West Norfolk and Wisbech AHA [1985]
UKHL 7 (17 October 1985)*. [online] Available at: www.bailii.
org/uk/cases/UKHL/1985/7.html. [Accessed 21 September
2020].

Criminal Justice Act 2003. [online] Available at: www.legislation.
gov.uk/ukpga/2003/44/part/13/crossheading/outraging-
public-decency [Accessed 18 September 2020].

Gadd, M. and Hinchliffe, J. (2007). *Jiwsi – A Pick 'n' Mix of Sex and
Relationships Education Activities*. [online] fpa.org. London:
FPA. Available at: www.fpa.org.uk/sites/default/files/jiwsi-sre-
activities-english.pdf [Accessed 18 September 2020].

Hambach, A., Evers, S., Summ, O., Husstedt, I.W. and Frese, A.
(2013). The impact of sexual activity on idiopathic headaches:
An observational study. *Cephalalgia*. [online] 33(6), 384–389.
Available at: https://doi.org/10.1177/0333102413476374
[Accessed 18 September 2020].

Human Rights Act 1998. [online] Available at: www.legislation.gov.
uk/ukpga/1998/42/schedule/1/part/I/chapter/7 [Accessed 18
September 2020].

Mental Capacity Act 2005. [online] Available at: www.legislation.gov.uk/ukpga/2005/9/section/1 [Accessed 18 September 2020].

Mental Health Act 2007. [online] Available at: www.legislation.gov.uk/ukpga/2007/12/part/1/chapter/1/crossheading/mental-disorder [Accessed 18 September 2020].

Rider, J.R., Wilson, K.M., Sinnott, J.A., Kelly, R.S., Mucci, L.A. and Giovannucci, E.L. (2016). Ejaculation frequency and risk of prostate cancer: Updated results with an additional decade of follow-up. [online] *European Urology*, 70(6), 974–982. Available at: www.europeanurology.com/article/S0302-2838(16)00377-8/fulltext [Accessed 18 September 2020].

Robbins, C.L. (2011). Prevalence, frequency, and associations of masturbation with partnered sexual behaviors among US adolescents. *Archives of Pediatrics & Adolescent Medicine* 165(12), 1087. [online] Available at: https://jamanetwork.com/journals/jamapediatrics/fullarticle/1107656.

Sex Education Forum (2011). *Parents and SRE: A Sex Education Forum Evidence Briefing.* [online] Available at: www.sexeducationforum.org.uk/sites/default/files/field/attachment/SRE and parents - evidence - 2011.pdf [Accessed 24 September 2020].

Sexual Offences Act 2003. [online] Available at: www.legislation.gov.uk/ukpga/2003/42/contents [Accessed 18 September 2020].

Sexual Offences (Northern Ireland) Order 2008. [online] Available at: www.legislation.gov.uk/nisi/2008/1769/contents [Accessed 18 September 2020].

Sexual Offences (Scotland) Act 2009. [online] Available at: www.legislation.gov.uk/asp/2009/9/contents [Accessed 6 December 2019].

Tenga (2019). *2019 Self-Pleasure Report: How Brits Masturbate and its Role in Self-Care.* [online] Available at: www.feelmore.global/wp-content/uploads/2019/05/TENGA-BCW-2019-Global-Survey-UK-Report-5.10.19.pdf [Accessed 18 September 2020].

World Health Organization (2018). *Defining Sexual Health*. World Health Organization. [online] Available at: www.who.int/reproductivehealth/topics/sexual_health/sh_definitions/en.

Further Reading

Adults with Incapacity (Scotland) Act 2000. [online] Available at: www.legislation.gov.uk/asp/2000/4 [Accessed 21 September 2020].

Age of Legal Capacity (Scotland) Act 1991. [online] Available at: www.legislation.gov.uk/ukpga/1991/50/section/2 [Accessed 21 September 2020].

Cambridge, P., Carnaby, S. and McCarthy, M. (2003). Responding to masturbation in supporting sexuality and challenging behaviour in services for people with learning disabilities. *Journal of Learning Disabilities*, 7(3), 251–266.

Council for the Curriculum, Examinations & Assessment (2015). *Relationships and Sexuality Education Guidance: An Update for Post-Primary Schools*. [online] Available at: https://ccea.org. uk/downloads/docs/ccea-asset/Curriculum/Relationships and Sexuality Education Guidance An Update for Post-Primary Schools.pdf [Accessed 19 September 2020].

Counsel, P. (2015). Criminal Justice and Courts Bill. [online] UK Parliament. Available at: https://publications.parliament.uk/pa/bills/lbill/2014-2015/0049/lbill_2014-20150049_en_5.htm [Accessed 22 September 2020].

Crown Prosecution Service (2019). Extreme Pornography. [online] Available at: www.cps.gov.uk/legal-guidance/extreme-pornography.

Department for Education (2019). *Relationships Education, Relationships and Sex Education (RSE) and Health Education*. [online] Available at: https://assets.publishing.service.gov. uk/government/uploads/system/uploads/attachment_data/ file/908013/Relationships_Education__Relationships_and_Sex_ Education__RSE__and_Health_Education.pdf.

Department of Education (2015). Relationships and sexuality education. [online] Available at: www.education-ni.gov.uk/ articles/relationships-and-sexuality-education [Accessed 24 November 2019].

Mental Capacity Act (Northern Ireland) 2016. [online] Available at: www.legislation.gov.uk/nia/2016/18/contents/enacted.

Mental Health (Care and Treatment) (Scotland) Act 2003. [online] Available at: www.legislation.gov.uk/asp/2003/13/contents.

National Archives (2019). Open Government Licence. [online] Available at: www.nationalarchives.gov.uk/doc/open- government-licence/version/3.

NSPCC Learning (2020). Gillick competence and Fraser guidelines. [online] Available at: https://learning.nspcc.org.uk/child- protection-system/gillick-competence-fraser-guidelines.

Scottish Government (2014). Conduct of relationships, sexual health and parenthood education in schools. [online] Available at: www.gov.scot/publications/conduct-relationships-sexual- health-parenthood-education-schools [Accessed 19 September 2020].

Welsh Government (2010). *Sex and Relationships Education in Schools*. [online] Available at: https://hwb.gov.wales/api/ storage/fb82a7b3-c88a-4473-a0b2-80fb2395b872/sex-and- relationships-education-in-schools.pdf [Accessed 19 September 2020].

Welsh Government (2019). *Relationships and Sexuality Education in Schools*. [online] Available at: https://gov.wales/sites/ default/files/consultations/2019-02/relationships-and-sexuality- education-in-schools-guidance.pdf [Accessed 19 September 2020].

Resources

There are useful resources that we can use to help us with masturbation and people with learning disabilities, and many are listed below. However, the most valuable resource is yourself and your willingness to talk about masturbation. Most of my sessions with young people and adults with learning disabilities are done with little more than flipchart paper and pens. I also use photographs of locations and activities for public and private sessions (see the chapter on masturbation education activities). I adapt my resources for the needs and abilities of all the people I work with, whether they have a learning disability or not. I ensure that my resources are as inclusive as possible and have a wide range of people represented.

It is useful to ask these questions to help you decide if a resource is going to be useful to you:

- What age is the resource for?
- How inclusive is the resource? Does it show a range of different people? Does it show people of different ethnicities? Does it include people with physical impairments? Is it inclusive for transgender people and different sexual orientations?
- Is it suitable if the person has a physical or sensory impairment? How could it be adapted?

- Must you be able to read? If you don't read, how can the resource be adapted?
- Is the resource visual enough for non-readers or readers of different languages?
- Can it be used by the person with learning disabilities on their own?
- How could you use this resource most effectively?

Capacity

Capacity to Consent to Sexual Relations
British Psychological Society (May 2019)
Overview of the legal framework and some common issues surrounding consent, sex and people with impaired capacity.
www.bps.org.uk

Exploring Sexual and Social Understanding (second edition)
Karen Dodd (2007, BILD Publications)
A capacity assessment pack for working with people with learning disabilities.
www.bild.org.uk

Sexual Knowledge and Behaviour Assessment Tool
Developed and written by the Revd Jane Fraser, edited by Hilary Dixon
This resource is for assessing levels of sexual knowledge and understanding of someone with a learning disability before and after a programme of relationship and sex education.
www.bodysense.org.uk

Law

Learning Disabilities Sex and the Law: A Practical Guide
Claire Fanstone and Sarah Andrews (2009, FPA)

How the law relates to work with people with learning disabilities.
https://fpa.org.uk

Masturbation

Intimate and Personal Care with People with Learning Disabilities
Steven Carnaby and Paul Cambridge (2006, Jessica Kingsley Publishers)
A guide to the management and practice of intimate and personal care for people with learning disabilities.

Masturbation – A Hands-On Guide
Jack Lukkerz and RFSU
A booklet about masturbation and how to masturbate.
www.rfsu.se

Sex and Masturbation
CHANGE
Easy-read book covering what sex and masturbation are.
www.changepeople.org

Sex for One: The Joy of Selfloving
Betty Dodson (1996, Random House Value Publications)
Betty explores her relationship with masturbation and sex, and works with other women to achieve improved sexual pleasure.

Things Ellie Likes: A Book About Sexuality and Masturbation for Girls and Young Women with Autism and Related Conditions
Kate E. Reynolds (2015, Jessica Kingsley Publishers)
Easy-read guide to masturbation and public/private.

Things Tom Likes: Sexuality and Masturbation for Boys and Young Men with Autism and Related Conditions
Kate E. Reynolds (2015, Jessica Kingsley Publishers)
Easy-read guide to masturbation and public/private.

Models and puppets
Condom demonstrator
A blue plastic penis model for condom education. Also useful for masturbation education.
https://fpa.org.uk

Daisy and Desmond
A range of anatomical models and cloth puppets for use in RSE.
www.bodysense.org.uk

Vulva and penis models
Anatomically exact educational models of vulvas and penises.
https://positivesexed.org

Wider relationships and sex education
All about Us (DVD-ROM)
A self-study learning tool that can be used by someone with learning disabilities on their own, or with support, to introduce key RSE issues.
https://fpa.org

Books Beyond Words
Books with no words addressing issues such as relationships, sexual abuse and sexual health.
www.booksbeyondwords.co.uk

CHANGE accessible booklets
A series of booklets: *Sex and Masturbation, My Pregnancy, My Choice, Parenting, You and Your Baby, You and Your Child, Friendships and Relationships, LGBTQ+, Safe Sex and Contraception, Understanding Sexual Abuse.*
www.changepeople.org

Great Relationships and Sex Education: 200+ Activities for Educators Working with Young People
Alice Hoyle and Ester McGeeny (2019, Routledge)
Creative RSE activities and session ideas.

Jiwsi – A Pick 'n' Mix of Sex and Relationships Education Activities
Mel Gadd and Jo Hinchliffe (2007, FPA)
A bilingual (English and Welsh) selection of adaptable RSE group-work activities.
Available as a free download from: sexeducationcompany.org and https://fpa.org

Makaton sex education signs and symbols
Makaton signs and symbols for RSE terms, including masturbation signs and symbols
https://makaton.org

Picture Yourself 1 & 2
Hilary Dixon and Ann Craft, illustrations by David Gifford (2004/2006, BodySense)
Sets of line drawings and photographs for use in sex and relationships work.
www.bodysense.org.uk

Sex and the 3 Rs – Rights, Risks and Responsibilities
Michelle McCarthy and David Thompson (2007, Pavilion)
A sex education package for people with learning disabilities.
www.pavpub.com

Sexuality and Learning Disabilities: A handbook, second edition
Bates, C. (2017, Pavilion)
www.pavpub.com

Sexuality and Severe Autism: A Practical Guide for Parents, Caregivers and Health Educators.
Kate E. Reynolds (2014, Jessica Kingsley Publishers)

Talking Together...About Sex and Relationships
Lorna Scott and Lesley Kerr-Edwards (2010, FPA)
https://fpa.org

Transgender Easy Read Guide
Developed by Choice Support, CMG and CHANGE (2019); An easy-read guide on sex and gender, being transgender and signposting to organizations that can help people transitioning.
www.choicesupport.org.uk

You, Your Body and Sex; *Jason's Private World*; and *Kylie's Private World*
Three DVD resources for working with people with learning disabilities.
https://lifesupportproductions.co.uk

Pornography
Online Pornography and Illegal Content – An Easy Read Guide
Developed by Care Management Group, CHANGE and Choice Support.
www.choicesupport.org.uk

Puberty and growing up

The Body Book
Claire Rayner (revised edition 1994, Scholastic)
An accessible book with illustrations explaining functions and
life stages of the human body.

Speakeasy: Talking with Your Children About Growing Up
FPA (2009)
How to answer children's questions about growing up,
relationships and sex.
https://fpa.org

Talking Together...About Growing Up
Lorna Scott and Lesley Kerr-Edwards (2010, FPA)
A book for parents and young people with learning
disabilities exploring puberty
https://fpa.org

*When Young People with Intellectual Disabilities and Autism
Hit Puberty: A Parents' Q&A Guide to Health, Sexuality and
Relationships*
Freddy Jackson Brown and Sarah Brown (2016, Jessica
Kingsley Publishers)

Organizations and websites

BISH
Practical RSE resources and information for young people
aged 14+.
www.bishuk.com

Brook
Sexual health charity providing education, advice and
services for under-25s.
www.brook.org.uk

CHANGE UK
Learning disability rights charity.
www.changepeople.org

Supported Loving
National network supporting professionals from all
backgrounds surrounding sexuality and intimate relationships
and people with a learning disability.
www.supportedloving.org.uk

Cwmni Addysg Rhyw – Sex Education Company
Social enterprise delivering RSE training and projects for
young people, people with learning disabilities and staff.
sexeducationcompany.org

FPA (Family Planning Association)
Relationships and sexual health publications and resources.
https://fpa.org.uk

Mencap
Charity for people with learning disabilities and their families.
www.mencap.org.uk

National Autistic Society
Charity for people with autism and their families.
www.autism.org.uk

NSPCC
Charity working to provide support and information to
prevent the abuse of children.
www.nspcc.org.uk

Thinkuknow
Online safety education and information for young people.
https://thinkuknow.co.uk

Index